Bow Wow the Dog Girl

By

Cindy Koch-Krol

Acknowledgements

I'd like to thank all of my Beta Readers, especially Victor and Sharon Vreeland, and Terise Gavar and her granddaughter Lily. As always I can't do this without my supportive family, Jeff and Jake, and my dear friends who must put up with me constantly telling them bits of the story line. Mostly, I thank my readers who have become staunch fans of my work. You know who you are!

Thank you,
Cindy Koch-Krol
5/29/18

Cathryn

Denise Kucher held her newborn in her arms, her bearded husband bending over them both.

His shirt had paint stains, his pants had spots of dried paint, and even his face was dotted. He had been working when Denise called out of the studio to tell him it was time. He dropped his paint brush and palate on the work table and pulled the car around at once.

"What are you going to call her?" the nurse asked.

"Her name is Cathryn after my grandmother," Denise said, her eyes never leaving the precious baby girl.

"Look at this face. She's as pretty as a bow," her father said. He looked up into his wife's eyes. "That's what I'm going to call her. Bow!"

That nickname stuck to me, like gorilla glue, and I never minded it. In fact the first day of school when the teacher took roll call, they would always call out my actual name, Cathryn Kucher, and I would correct them and tell them that I go by Bow. That is, until high school.

In high school everyone has something to prove. Most of us need to prove we are smart, or talented in some way, some of us have to prove we are good athletes. We all have to prove that we are better at something than someone else or we're nobody.

It was easy to see that nearly everyone else was better than me.

When I looked in the mirror on the day I started high school I realized that puberty had done nothing for me. I had been a pretty little girl with lots of friends. Now I'm a gawky pimply-faced misfit with glasses and braces. I was taller than most of the boys in junior high. I had bigger bones than most of the girls. They all seemed to be such delicate little flowers next to my clunky awkward frame. My hands were the size of dinner plates, and my feet were so huge that I had to wear boy's shoes. My mother just shook her head and told me I was imagining all of this. After all, her feet were the same way. She and I wore the same shoe size.

She leaned her chin on my shoulder as we both looked in the mirror. “Don’t worry, all your friends will catch up with you.”

I turned my head to kiss her cheek. Her skin was dry, there were dark bags under her eyes, and her cheekbones showed already. They hadn’t shown this much since the last time she had relapsed.

Mom was diagnosed when I was in second grade. She fought the disease with all her might but in the end her only recourse was a devastating surgery. The surgery removed the cancer and she only needed one round of Chemo before it was gone, undetectable. Of course we were told that it was no guarantee. She always knew she might relapse.

My father left us when it became apparent that he couldn’t deal with my mother’s altered body. I’m not saying that he divorced her because she was sick. But he couldn’t handle it. Mom told me that after the surgery he didn’t treat her like a woman anymore, whatever that means.

My father was the kind of person that needed to have beautiful and lively people around him at all times. And, well, my mother had breast cancer.

My family was dying, and I could do nothing but watch.

But lately it had been good. I had been raised with a long series of rescue dogs. In retrospect I can now see that she didn't want to just straight up adopt a dog because she knew if she ever got sick again she wouldn't be able to take care of it, and up until this year, I was too young to be totally responsible for a pet. But we had fun with the rescue dogs. Mom had a kennel built in our backyard to accommodate them with an indoor shelter where they could go to get in out the weather. If it got too cold or rainy or nasty out we would always bring them in the house, but for those days with mild wind or cold they could huddle up together in the shelter for warmth.

I tried not to get attached to them, but they were so hurt and pathetic that I couldn't help myself. I would cry when we gave them to their new forever homes.

One time a mother with two boys came to adopt one of our dogs. We had four dogs at that time. Three were being housed in the kennel and one was a timid little Lhasa-Apso that Mom was looking after in the house. When they came into the house, the Lhasa-Apso, whose name was Ginger, came out of hiding briefly to look at the new family. The youngest boy, who was about 8, lunged toward her and she scampered back toward the bedroom.

"Well, let me take you out to meet the dogs," Mom said cheerfully. I had been about to scold the boy for making that quick of a move toward the small dog. She had only begun to trust Mom, and she still didn't trust me yet. So I knew that this was not the dog for this family with two active boys.

"You should take Rufus," I told the woman as she looked around the yard.

The three dogs had come up to the edge of the kennel to greet us with exuberant barking as they always did, and I could tell that the mother was a little frightened.

"Rufus is really friendly, and he's very well adjusted. He'll play nicely with your boys and be a good companion for them," Mom said.

"Oh my gosh, he's so big!" the woman said. "I think we need a smaller dog."

I felt the need to second my mom's opinion. I felt very strongly about this, I don't know why. "Rufus would never hurt anyone. He's just a big fluffy ball of love and affection. He doesn't even bark that much. He's real active and I think your boys need a dog that's more active and can stand up to rough housing."

The mother kept her eyes on Rufus like she didn't entirely trust him not to lunge at her. "I kind of like that little one in the house. Is that one up for adoption?"

Mom called Rufus over to her. The Shepard/boxer mix stood about thigh high on their youngest boy.

“Oh, he is way too big,” the woman said. “I just don’t think the boys will respond to him. They might be afraid of him.”

I gave my mother a look. She returned it. We both knew who exactly was afraid of big dogs.

“Bow, why don’t you get Rufus out of the kennel so the boys can play with him for a while?"

Mom led the woman back into the house where they could speak in private.

I showed the boys how Rufus likes to play. I threw a tennis ball and Rufus fetched it and then we had a little tug of war with a knotted rope. The boys took right over and began to play with him, rolling on the ground and wrestling with him. Rufus seemed to instinctively know that these boys meant him no harm and because of that he let them do whatever they wanted, including pulling his ears, and falling over his back, trying to ride him like a horse, other stuff like that. I could tell that Rufus was making a love connection with these boys and he was becoming their dog. He started licking the face of the younger one and the boy couldn’t stop giggling at the feel of the rough tongue on his chin and cheeks. He was only able to get Rufus to stop by hugging him tightly so his mouth was over the boys shoulder.

The family left with Ginger.

A few days later, Mom got a phone call from the mother.

"You were right. This dog is just too timid. She hides, and doesn't come out until she knows the boys are gone. I've tried to tell the boys to be calm and try to coax the dog out of hiding with treats, but when she comes out she is shaking like a leaf. My younger son told me last night that he hates that dog. I'm afraid I'm going to have to bring it back to you. She's not happy and we're not happy, the whole situation is making the family miserable."

"Yes, I knew it was a bad match. But I'm not supposed to refuse any offer of a good home for our rescue dogs. And yours is a very good home for the right dog. Bring her back. We'll see if we can't come to another arrangement."

When they came back Mom took Ginger back into the house where she stayed under the safety of the bed for three days. Meanwhile, the boys began playing with Rufus as soon as they got out of the car. Rufus was a pretty smart dog I guess because at one point he ignored the boys and walked up to their mother. He sniffed at her hand and then ducked his head under it so she couldn't help but pet him.

"Oh my," she said. "You are a friendly creature."

"He's really smart and trainable too, he's already house trained," I told her. "I've been working with him on the leash too. I'm sure he will follow your instructions on walks and the like. He's not an alpha dog at all. He'll bend over backward to please you."

She shook her head. "Don't you have a smaller dog than Rufus that likes to play? He's going to make such a mess in the yard."

I looked at my Mom again. But she didn't notice because she was laughing.

"Just because he's a bigger dog doesn't mean he's going to make a bigger mess. All dogs leave messes in the yard. If you want I can send my daughter over to your house to train him to only go in one section of your yard so you don't have to go on an Easter egg hunt with the honey dipper."

"You can do that?" she asked.

This was the clincher! The boys got their dog and Rufus got a forever home.

After that, Mom took my instincts to heart when placing dogs with people.

Ginger was adopted by a fifty year old widow woman who sold her home and spent her retirement years driving around in her RV. Ginger was the perfect companion dog for her gentle touch and exercise level.

Mom taught me everything about training dogs. That lesson took only about five minutes.

"Just tell them clearly what you expect of them and when they don't do it correct them gently. When they do it, praise them greatly. Once they see you as the alpha dog, they will always see you as the alpha dog. That's when you can let them off the hook and allow them to play and sniff and be who they are. You don't always have to be in control."

It occurred to me that that's kind of how she raised me as well. Dogs just want to be loved. And they want to love their people too. So they are always trying to please their people. Humans are like that too.

For years I've gone with mom to get her tests done. Each time they came back in the clear we would celebrate with a trip to our favorite restaurant, Hill's Fish Shack. She loved their crab cakes, and I loved the fried perch.

Mom's appointment was scheduled for my first full day of high school, so I couldn't go with her. But I knew that if it was good news we would have two things to celebrate tonight at the Fish Shack.

I was excited to start high school. I had that brand new feeling that everyone gets on the first day of the new school year. I wanted to learn so much. I wanted to take all the different classes and learn everything there was to learn.

On the first day of school, I walked into my science class room and saw a boy I knew.

He was one of Rufus' boys. I thought, hey, someone I actually know! I went up to him to say hi. He turned and looked at me. He was with four other boys. They were all wearing the same T-shirts denoting that they were all members of the J.V. football squad.

His face lit up when he saw me. "Hey it's the dog girl."

One of his friends stepped between us.

"Dog girl?" the second one said. "Go away dog girl."

They began to laugh, and I saw sadness and even a little pity come into the eyes of Rufus' boy.

I turned, disappointed to have not made a friend, and I sat near the back of the room. The J.V. boys all sat up front.

But when Mom picked me up after school that day, I didn't tell her about Rufus' boy and the other J.V. boys. I could tell that something was wrong.

"It's just a small spot," she told me. "The doctors have every hope that the treatments will work."

"Mom, don't lie to me. This is ME!"

"I'm not lying. I know you can handle the truth. I'm telling you the truth."

"You're not telling everything," I accused.

"No, true, I'm not. But I choose to celebrate the small victories this time. I AM going to see you graduate! I will not leave you until you can be on your own."

"Mom," I said. She could hear the anguish in my voice.

"NO," she said sternly. "We aren't going to do this pity party thing. We still have each other and we still will be able to do what we do. Small victories."

I wanted to hear her say everything would be alright. I wouldn't lose her. I wouldn't have to rely on my deadbeat father, ever. I didn't even know where my father was. I had a phone number that the court had given me and I sent thank you notes to him through the court on those rare occasions that I got a birthday card or Christmas gift from him. He had not been in touch personally in over five years. Mom told me that he had a new wife, and soon I heard that he also had a new family.

At the end of that first week of school, we had a test in Science. I wanted to make all A's, and this test would be my proving ground. The teacher warned us that there would be a bonus question. She hinted that if we kept up with the reading and even read ahead a little, we would know the answer to the bonus question. I read as far ahead in the text as I could that first week and took careful notes.

I did great on the test! The bonus question had to do with the next chapter we would be studying. That was it. Anyone who looked at the title of the next chapter would have gotten it right. But I had read the entire chapter, so—bonus!

On Monday we got the tests back, and under my name on the top of the test the teacher had written, “A+ WOW!”

I had written my name as Bow Kucher. When she handed back the tests she gave it to the first person in the row who handed it back through the row to the person it belonged to. One of the J.V. guys got my paper and read the top of it.

“Bow Wow? Bow Wow Kucher the dog girl!” he said.

The other boys laughed.

“Bow Wow the dog girl,” he taunted.

I tried to hide behind my books, but it didn’t work. The teacher brought the class to order with a stern look, but I knew that wouldn’t be the end of it.

At lunch time the J.V. boys made such a big deal about calling me Bow Wow that everyone in the Cafeteria caught on. I couldn’t escape it, that was now my nickname.

Lance

My dad is an astronaut. I always lead with that fact because that's what I want to be too.

Knowing that my dad was an astronaut, all of my heroes were astronauts. My dad bought me an autograph book when I was four. All of the astronauts on his crew signed it for me. I was in awe of this and people told me that if I kept collecting autographs in that little book that someday it would be worth a lot of money.

When I was four, ten dollars was a lot of money. So I suspected that if I had every astronaut's autograph, I would someday have at least ten dollars. Stupid huh?

That was the same year as the Challenger crash. My dad had flown a shuttle mission a few months earlier and that's when he had gotten me the autograph book. So I begged him to let me go to the launch party for the Challenger mission. I was allowed to go down the row with my sharpie marker and have each of the astronauts sign my book, including mission specialist and teacher Christa McAuliffe. I remember her especially because she got down on her knees to talk with me. She asked me what I wanted to be when I grew up. I told her I wanted to be an astronaut like my dad.

She smiled at me. "You know, I think you will. Maybe you'll be the first man to walk on Mars!"

I think my grin stayed in place for the next full hour. But then we watched the launch.

Within two minutes after lift-off there was an explosion. I saw it happen with my own two eyes. First a rocket with flames spurting out the back trying to break out of the Earth's atmosphere, and then billows of smoke going in three different directions. I heard my father gasp. I stood gape-mouthed and the only thing I could think about was the seven names written in my autograph book.

"Where are the astronauts?" I asked Dad. He would not answer. "Where did they go? Dad? Are they OK?"

He could not answer. No one answered that question. Ever!

After that my oldest brother, Steve, stopped telling people that he wanted to be an astronaut, and he made us stop saying it too. I still wanted to be an astronaut, more than anything. I wanted to prove that I could do it, just the way Christa McAuliffe had said. I would be the first man to stand on Mars! That was still my goal, whether my brother let me say it or not.

With those seven famous names in my book, along with the eight less famous names of my dad's crew who didn't die, I began to carry the book with me every time I went on the base. I always asked everyone if they were an astronaut. If the answer was yes, they would sign my book. People would do anything for a four, five or even a six year old kid. It wasn't until I was seven or eight before they would disregard me as being unimportant and stopped signing my book. But by that time I had every shuttle astronaut in my book, and most of the rocket jockeys. When I was ten I was able to meet John Glen who was a senator by then. He came to a special dedication event in Huston and Dad pulled some strings to get me the chance to ask for his autograph. His was the last one I needed of the original seven Mercury Astronauts. Of course, I could only have six of the seven sign my actual book. Gus Grissom died before I was born. But I still had his autograph pasted in my book. Dad had found an old receipt that he had signed, and asked me if I wanted it.

Growing up in Houston as the family of an astronaut, there were always people around. Reporters looking for interviews, science groupies, experimenters, fans. They stopped mom in the grocery store, they knocked on our door. One even stopped me from being grounded.

Mom came into the living room one time and found me on the floor flat on my butt. I had knocked over an end table and a lamp with a ceramic base, smashed it to bits and dented the lamp shade. I don't think the table was in that great of shape either. It kind of wobbled after that. Mom came in guns blazing. She was about to verbally abuse me, send me to my room and probably ground me, even though I had not, of my own volition, propelled myself into this situation. But my older brothers had been able to make good their escape while I was recovering my senses and wondering if I was seriously injured. The only thing that saved me was the doorbell.

A group of fans had found our house and wanted to know, "What is it like to . . ." whatever. I got the heck out of there as fast as I could. By the time Mom got around to punishing me, she no longer had the heart for it.

Dad was always gone. When he wasn't on mission he was away doing propaganda. Oh, excuse me, Public Relations programs. He would go to high schools around the country and talk, or give radio interviews, especially before a mission. All this was to give the public confidence in what NASA was continuing to do, especially in the changing climate, where people thought the government should be spending money to make their own lives better, rather than spending it on sending rockets into orbit.

To make up for all the crap we had to put up with, Dad would buy us stuff. He wouldn't give us everything we wanted, but he would usually buy us the second thing we asked for. This is how my older brothers both got Motorcycles, and my younger brothers got Mini bikes. I didn't want transportation, I was a runner. But I also knew I wasn't getting the first thing I asked for so at age 14 I asked for a car. Dad said no to the car, obviously. So I said, "OK, I want a dog. I want the biggest dog in the world."

"Why a big dog?" Dad asked me.

"So he can run with me."

I started running when I was in grade school. It took me away from my brothers and it made me faster than them. I ran track in junior high and got really good. The dog was the first thing—the only thing—I wanted.

"Brent," my mother said. "I'll be the one caring for it. I'll be the one cleaning up after it and feeding it. NO!"

"Come on," my Dad said. "He doesn't ask for anything much."

My Dad was good for his word. He got me the biggest dog he could find. It was a three year old pure bred Great Dane. We saved it from pound. According to the worker at the pound who handled our adoption, this dog had become bigger than the original owner had anticipated and she didn't want it anymore. He also said that the dog would need to be trained. He was a little on the unruly side. But I didn't anticipate what all that would entail.

In 8th grade, I had a growth spurt and stood five foot eleven. I was as tall as my two older brothers and faster because of my running. So the torture subsided a little.

That's the year Dad announced his retirement.

"We'll be moving back home to Michigan at the end of this school year."

"No!" Scott said. "I was going to play varsity football next year. This new school probably has a sucky football team."

Steve was right with him. "What about me? I have to make all new friends in my senior year? I have to find a new girlfriend before Prom?"

I didn't want to mention that if he really liked his current girlfriend he probably would not be so worried about finding a new one.

"I have five children," Dad said. "There is never going to be a perfect time to move, so we're just going to do it now and make the best of it."

"Home to Michigan?" I asked. "I've never even been to Michigan, why is that home?"

"Hey," Dad said. "Michigan is great. Water in Michigan has no salt or sharks. It's always fresh, sometimes frozen."

No one laughed.

"I grew up in Ann Arbor. You're going to love it."

I figured that if Dad was happy and quiet in Michigan that would be good. Maybe the surprise visits from space groupies would be brought down to a minimum.

At any rate, I had my dog Clyde, so my life couldn't suck that bad.

I was wrong.

Cathryn

I came home from school about a month into the freshman year and found mom on her knees slumped over the toilet.

There was puke all over her shirt front.

“Mom!” I said. “What happened?”

“I just got sick, and then I was so weak I couldn’t move.”

“Let me help you,” I said. I tried to get my arm around her to lift her up but she told me to let it be for a minute.

“Run me a bath, will you?” I did as she asked without hesitation. She literally crawled from the toilet to the bathtub and stopped there. She slid her jeans off and asked me to help pull them off. Then she lifted her arms and I slid the shirt off over her head trying to be careful not to let the vomit fall into her face or hair.

Her ribs were black with bruises caused by the violent retching.

"Mom!" I couldn't help it. I was shocked by the sight of my poor mother's condition.

"If I went to the ER they would think I was an abused wife," she said trying to smile.

"Not funny!" I told her.

She turned to slide her upper body into the warm water and then pulled her lower half in afterward. She did a half turn so she was again facing upward and lay back in the hot water.

"Too hot," I asked.

"No, actually it feels good."

"Tea?" I asked.

"No, just some water. I don't want to upset my stomach again."

I went to the kitchen and got some water. I yelled back to her to ask if she wanted ice in it or to leave it warm. I didn't get an answer. I went back into the bathroom and she had fallen asleep in the tub. She looked like a torture victim.

It hurt my heart to watch her go through this. I knew she was doing it for me. Her goal in life was to make it to my graduation so I wouldn't have to go into foster care.

What I didn't know at that time, was how resistant this new strand of cancer was to the treatments.

A few days later, when she was a bit more rested, I sat down at the dinner table with her to have our normal Wednesday night meal of spaghetti and garlic bread.

"Mom, the surgery worked before, can't you just have another surgery and get it all out of there at once?"

"That won't work this time. It's not just one lumpy mass now, there are spots in several places. It wouldn't take just one surgery, and it would be too easy to miss something. Chemo targets all the places with one massive dose of drugs that runs through my whole system and kills everything it can find."

"But it makes you so sick," I said. "Mom I hate seeing you like this."

"I know sweetie, but you have to be strong. In fact you have to get a lot stronger, because you have to survive this."

"You are the one that has to survive this," I said to her.

"No, I'm not going to survive this."

When she said this to me, I listened carefully. She had given me a book to read that told about the stages of grief. I think I went through each one of them in the few moments that passed after she said this.

"Of course you'll survive it. You have to, you're my mother."

"I am not going to survive this thing, honey. You have to accept that fact."

"But you said that you would be around to see me graduate."

"Yes, and hope I can last that long. But if I don't you still have to be prepared for what's to come."

"But mom, what can I do? I'll quit school and take care of you to make it easier for you. Maybe if I'm here all the time things will be easier and you can focus on healing."

"Nope, that's not going to cut it. You have a life to live and the only way you're going to be prepared to live it is if you stay in school and keep your grades up. You have to focus on your school work."

"But Mom, how am I going to do that, with you sick?"

"We'll find a way. You have to have a plan, get into a good college, and these plans have to be set in stone before I die. That way you won't be able to back out just because you're grieving a loss."

"Grieving a loss? Mom?"

"Yes. We will undoubtedly go through some grieving together, and by the end I want to make sure that you are in a frame of mind that you will be able to go on. You have to have a good plan, and it must be set in stone, and you will just go ahead with it automatically. I refuse to let you fall apart because of my death."

"But Mom."

"No! Too many bad things can happen to girls that have no plans and no support system in place. It's going to be very hard for you, but if we prepare ahead of time and plan this out wisely, you will get through it."

I stopped to really hear what she was saying. I was having a hard time imagining my life without her steady hand to guide me. I thought that maybe I needed to do as she suggested.

"What do you think my plan should be?" I asked.

"Well, I would hope college at first. Apply for no fewer than five. Decide which will be your safety college and make sure you get into that one. Then apply to other better colleges that you are not so sure about. Work hard, keep your grades up. Do some extracurricular activities. You know all this."

"I'll do track, and I'll do dog rescues, and I'll get a job walking dogs."

"I can't do dog rescues anymore," Mom said. "I don't have the energy. I can't take care of them like I used to."

"I can. I'll do it."

"No, they won't allow it. An adult has to be in charge. They wouldn't give me any dogs to care for being that I can't even take care of myself."

Our last dog had been adopted out just days after Mom told me she had relapsed. I missed having a dog.

"Forget about the dogs for now," Mom said. "You can have plenty of dogs in the future. Maybe dogs are your future. Maybe you should go to Michigan State, become a veterinarian."

I had thought about that. But mostly what vets do is euthanize. I didn't want that. I wanted to be a dog trainer. "Maybe I'll become a cop, work with dogs as a trainer. Maybe I can train dogs to be seeing-eye dogs."

"Maybe," mom said. "I would prefer it if you would plan to do something that was not quite so specialized and maybe a little more achievable in the short run. Like maybe teacher, or nurse. You can always switch out to a career in dog training once you have an income to stand on."

I could see what she meant. I had to think about my future in practicalities, not in abstract wishful thinking. I sat down and wrote two lists, dividing a page in half like a pro's and con's list. I listed the things that I wanted to do on one side and the things I thought I could do on the other.

The wanted to do side, was all about dogs. I wanted to walk dogs, train dogs, and be a dog owner. I wanted to keep running and run with dogs. I wanted to train dogs for police work, or for service dogs. I wanted to help dogs with their people problems, like that guy on TV. I could not see a future for myself that did not include dogs.

On the other side of the page, the side that said things I think I could do, I wrote my mom's two suggestions: nurse and teacher. Then I wrote, cook, waitress, lab technician, track coach, factory worker.

When I showed the list to my mom she said, "Do you know that you only have three professions on here that actually need a college degree? The others are just jobs that you can get right out of high school."

"I know, but they are all jobs that I wouldn't mind doing."

"Try for a college degree."

"I'd have a huge debt to start out with in life if I did that," I said.

"I have life insurance my dear. There will be enough to minimize any loans you may have to get. What's important now is that you get good grades because that will teach you how to get good grades in college."

"I can do it, Mom."

"No really," she said. "You have to get used to ignoring everything else but your school work. I'm going to continue to get sick. You can't let your grades slide because of me. Do you understand?"

I understood her entirely. I had never let my grades slide because of her illnesses. But then, I was still in grade school last time she was sick. Maybe the teachers made allowances. I didn't know at the time how bad it would get.

Things at school were getting worse. No one knew my actual name. Some of my teachers still called me Bow, but I had privately asked them all to call me Cathryn. It was time. I had outgrown my father's childish nickname.

One boy at school would not let the name drop though. Scott, the J.V. boy from my class, egged on by his cheerleader girlfriend, Lynn, kept the taunts going.

Lynn always seemed to be on Scott's arm, or at least within kissing length of his lips. So the day before the homecoming game, Lynn saw me in the hall and yelled out, "There she is, Scott."

His attention was drawn to my tall frame. I buried my head in the book and tried to walk past.

That was how I got my one and only friend that year.

Lance

My Dog, Clyde, came with a lot of problems.

We were all planning to fly to Michigan when we moved. But Clyde couldn't fly because there was no way to contain him. So Dad and I drove the station wagon to Michigan with Clyde in the back.

We had to put up a fence between the front seat and the back seat because otherwise he would just climb over and sit in my lap. It was a long grueling trip from Houston to Ann Arbor. We had to stop every two hours to let the dog out and give him some water.

He cried with discomfort nearly the entire way, and he pooped and peed in the car at least once per day despite the two hour exercise breaks.

When we got to Ann Arbor there were other problems. We quickly found that he couldn't have the run of the house and he was a regular Houdini when it came to opening doors and slipping out of his collar when it was attached to a chain.

On one hand I was happy I had such a smart dog, but on the other hand, I didn't want to risk losing him if someone opened the gate to the back yard by accident and let him out.

So Mom called the first week and had someone come over and build an eight foot high fenced in kennel for him. It had to have a special gate with a latch to push a dog bowl through otherwise he would have knocked me over when I fed him.

He was a special needs dog. On regular dog food he would start to get sick. He was allergic to something that they put in it. Nearly every dog food had this additive, whatever it was. We found this out when we took him to the new vet in Ann Arbor. He suggested a change in Clyde's diet.

Mom was very disturbed to hear this. Clyde's food had to be home cooked. He would thrive on home cooked beef or pork, He could also eat boneless chicken but only sometimes. He could eat nothing that came out of a can. He also liked vegetables to balance out his nutrition. He ate from a six quart steel mixing bowl. He couldn't eat or drink from a plastic bowl because he thought they were chew toys and would destroy them afterward.

We were warned to keep him away from feminine hygiene products. I thought the guy meant like mom's deodorant, but mom knew what he was talking about. Turns out Clyde liked eating tampons. He needed to stay away from anything made of leather. We gave him actual beef soup bones as chew toys and sometime natural pig skin ones. If I wanted to play fetch with him I had to make sure it was an old football that no one wanted anymore because he would crush it in his powerful jaws.

Clyde ate three pounds of meat per day, and it had to be cooked or he would get used to the raw flavor and he might start hunting his own meat. He would also eat one pound of carrots per day, a full head of broccoli or cauliflower, and a one pound bag of frozen peas. All of this had to be cooked until it was tender.

Every morning I got up an hour early to fix his meal. I washed the vegetables and cut them into chunks, threw everything into a roasting pan, including the meat and then set it in the fridge. When Mom came home from her volunteer work at around 2:00 P.M. she put the roasting pan in the oven. Then at 4:00 P.M. she would take it out to allow it to cool. I usually got home from practice around 5:00 P.M. By then it was cool enough to feed Clyde. I would chunk up the meat and mix it all up in the steel bowl and take it out to him in his kennel. He weighed 150 pounds and when he had the momentum he could knock down anyone he wanted. Me, carrying a big bowl of food, was child's play for him.

I found that I couldn't walk him. I had to run him. But I couldn't keep up with him, not even running. And God forbid if I ever had to stop, he would yank my arm out of my socket.

There was nothing I could do with this dog. Mom wouldn't allow him in the house, because he always made a mess and was constantly knocking things down with his tail. I would sometimes take him to my room, but I had to watch my soda. He would knock any drink glasses over just on general principle. He would find the most expensive thing in my room and chew on it: $100 Nike's, my football pads, my favorite CD's. Nothing was sacred.

I love my dog, don't get me wrong. He was very affectionate. He just was too destructive. It was always a fight between me and Mom, all the time. She wanted the dog in the kennel whenever I wasn't around to keep a strict eye on him. I wanted him to stay in my room whenever possible. Clyde had a mind of his own though.

He wouldn't do either thing. He learned to open the door of my bedroom and get out, leaving the door knob slick with dog spit.

Mom would grab him by the collar and try to get him into the kennel, but he outweighed her by 20 pounds, so he wouldn't go where she wanted him to go. She had to lure him with a soup bone to go into the kennel.

Meanwhile, life at school was vacillating between good and great. My two oldest brothers and I had come into school in June to try out for the football teams. Scott and I got onto the J.V. squad, Scott was unhappy about that. If he had stayed in Texas, he would have been on the varsity team.

Steve did get on the varsity, and within a few weeks of practices he was first string. Steve was a kick-ass player, always had been. He was 6'2", weighed 180 lbs. and could almost outrun me. He had all the natural raw talent and he had a football scholarship to Michigan State next year. Steve was a shoe-in to be the big high school football star.

Steve would pave the way for me and Scott. As his two younger brothers, we reaped the benefit of all our coaches knowing that our brother was a worthy player and therefore, we might be also.

Scott was two years ahead of me, a junior that first year. He was a good player too. He was actually better at baseball than football, but he played on both teams and the basketball team as well. I did too. I played football and basketball that first year, but instead of baseball, I ran track. Unlike other team sports, the track team got to work out with the girls.

My brothers both dated cheerleaders. Don’t get me wrong, the cheerleaders had good dance moves but they weren’t in as good shape as the track girls. Just saying!

Cathryn

Meg was a mousy little girl, about five foot nothing, with nondescript brown hair and skinny as a post. She too was a freshman and she was flat as a pancake. I didn't have a whole lot on top, but at least mine were round. Her boobs weren't even pointed yet. When my mom met her, she called Meg a late bloomer.

I was walking down the hall reading, this time for real. I heard across the hall, "Scott, there she is."

"Hey, Bow Wow," Scott called to me. I just kept walking, giving them the cold shoulder like I always did.

"Quick, she's getting away," Lynn told him.

I turned the corner to the science hallway. My next class was Earth Science. I kept my head down in my book, even though I was no longer reading.

"Leave her alone," one of the other football players said to him.

"Bow Wow, Here girl! Roll over! Here Bow Wow," he persisted, while his girlfriend giggled uproariously.

All at once, I heard him hit the floor behind me. He began to curse. I looked back to see what happened. The little mousy girl looked astonished.

"I'm sorry," she said. "I didn't mean to do that."

Scott had fallen flat on his face and bumped his chin on the floor. He must have bit his lip because it was bleeding.

"You did that on purpose you little creep," Lynn yelled.

"I didn't, I didn't even see him coming up behind me. It was an accident."

Lynn faced the smaller girl and pushed her hard against the lockers. Lynn's face was uglier than I had ever seen it before. "Get out of my face, you little nobody."

Meg grabbed her book out of her locker and hurried to close it. Then she came down the hall toward me. When we were out of sight of the main hall and the jocks stationed there, Meg caught up to me.

"That was close," she said. She was smiling.

"Did she push you?" I asked her.

"Yeah, but she didn't hurt me. I've taken worse." I looked down at this plucky little girl and her wide friendly smile. I decided that I liked her.

"You shouldn't have to take that," I told her.

Her smile disappeared for a few seconds replaced with a grave look. "Neither should you." But her smile was back in an instant, "Besides, I did him a favor. He doesn't have to go see his drug dealer today because he's already had a good trip!"

I laughed and she laughed with me.

When I got out of class 50 minutes later, she was waiting for me.

"Can we hang out after school?"

"I usually go for a run after school and get something to eat."

"Oh, well, how about tomorrow at lunch time?"

"I usually go to the library during lunch time," I told her.

"I usually eat down in the stairwell, behind the auto shop. No one bothers me down there."

"Do a lot of people bother you?" I asked.

"Same crew that bothers you. Only I don't make it fun for them like you do. I give back what they give me."

"How?"

"They call me Minnie Mouse, I call them Dumbo or Goofy, or Daffy Duck. They call me nerd or dweeb, I call them Neanderthal or troglodyte. Whatever they do I give it back to them only worse. A couple of them have given up on me. But he was going to come up behind you and knock your books out of your hands. He was about to get physical with you, so I tripped him. It was so funny. You should have seen his face."

I smiled. "I wish I could have. I just always hope that if I don't react at all they will get bored and leave me alone."

"Naw, they hate you too much for that."

"See, why? Why should they hate me? I never did anything to them."

"You get good grades, you're pretty, you're tall, and you have a nice body."

"I'm pimply and I have glasses and braces."

"We're teenagers, we all have zits. You're teeth actually look pretty straight, you're going to get out of your braces soon I would think."

"Next summer," I confirmed.

"Then all you'll need is some contacts and a bottle of acne medication."

"I'm too big to be a cheerleader and too uncoordinated."

"So, who cares? That girl—Lynn—just hates you because she can see that even with your braces and your glasses your prettier than she is. But then again, I tend to see people who are nice as being beautiful. She's a witch underneath and it kind of taints her beauty."

I knew exactly what she was talking about. I felt the same way only I had never had the words to say it like that.

Meg smiled at me and I could tell at once, that even though she was short and maybe had not hit puberty yet, she was a very pretty girl.

When I met Meg, I stood more than 8 inches taller than her, but we were still best friends. When I went out for the girls track team in spring, she did too. She had a natural runner's body. She could run distances, but she couldn't run very fast. She got faster as her legs grew stronger over the course of the track season. But more important, this started us on a trend in our friendship. Nearly as soon as we became friends we wanted to do everything together.

Mom finished her round of chemo around the time Meg and I started training for track. By the time our first track meet was held she was feeling good enough to come out and attend. I drove her as close as I could to the bleachers and then parked the car. Afterward, I went back for the car and picked her up. She didn't have the stamina to walk from the parking lot herself. I came in second in the 440, and third in the 220 that day.

We had plenty of time between bouts because the boys were running in the same meet. We trained together with the boys and some of the girls were dating the boys we ran with. Most of the boys were also on other sports teams including the football team. So I was not going to purposely mix with any of them.

By the time the last track meet came around Mom had gone to the doctor again and there were still signs of the tumor in her rib. She needed a round of radiation next. Mom told me to expect this, but I was still concerned.

"Don't worry," she said. "I will be back in remission again by the end of this round of treatments."

When Meg found out about my mom, she became very concerned. She told me she had talked about it with her parents.

"Really? What did you say?"

"I told them that your mother wanted to see you graduate and that she didn't think she would last too much longer than that."

"What did they say?"

"Mom got all concerned and wanted to know if we should invite the two of you over for dinner to get to know you."

"Um, is that all?" I asked.

"Well, yeah, for now. I think that's her way of opening up a friendship with your mom so that she can maybe become part of her support system. My mom is big on support systems."

"That would be great," I said. But at the same time I didn't know what my mom would think. Mom was totally into a mentality of "we can do this ourselves." But to be honest, lately I felt like I needed more support than that.

"You know what I think we ought to do?" Meg asked me.

"What?"

"I think we should enroll in summer school and get a couple of credit hours this summer. Maybe if we do that we could graduate early."

"And Mom wouldn't have so long to wait?" I asked. Meg said nothing. There was nothing to say. It occurred to both of us at the same time that if we graduated early then Mom might be free to die earlier too. I sighed.

"It doesn't mean we HAVE to graduate early just that we can if we needed to. You know?"

Then I saw what she was getting at. It wasn't that mom *could* die sooner, but if she *did* die sooner then I wouldn't have to spend that last semester in high school. I could graduate early and get on with my life.

So we both signed up for English Literature and American Studies during summer school. We spent all morning in school and there were no football players to torture us. It was great.

Since our classes were over by noon, we had all afternoon to ourselves. But we couldn't go shopping or out to see a movie because we had no money between us. So we applied for jobs at the ice cream shop. The owner, a wonderful woman named Naomi, hired us both and, at our request, gave us the same shifts. She liked us I think, because there were very few times that I worked when Meg didn't, and vice versa. We got afternoon or evening shifts at least three of them each week.

Meg told me that Mom and I were invited over to her house for dinner on Friday night because her parents wanted to get to know us. I told Mom about it and she said, "Sure. I think it's about time, don't you?"

I thought she meant about time we got to know Meg's parents. But later I thought maybe she meant that it was about time she got some actual friends of her own.

"Denise, I'm so happy you could make it," Meg's Mom said. She gave her a big hug and didn't let go for a long time.

Meg's dad just shook her hand.

"I know you," Mom said to him. "You work at Huntington don't you?"

"Yeah, I'm a loan officer there," he said.

"Investments, Savings and Loan."

"Oh, yes, of course, I saw you at the Savings and Loan convention last year, right?" he said. "Jack Bennett."

Go figure, my mom and Meg's dad had something in common.

"Right," she said.

He stood awkwardly for a moment and then announced, "I will now, attack the backyard grill, and make sure the proper amount of char is put onto the ribs. The rest of the family is in the kitchen," he said, then directed us toward that room. Of course, I knew where it was. I'd only been hanging out here for six months.

Meg was tossing a salad, and Meg's mom, Grace, was cutting up potatoes into julienne style fries.

After some pleasant conversation, Mr. Bennett asked us kids if we wanted to go see a movie—his treat. We all agreed and we went to find a paper to see if there was one that we could all see, that was still appropriate for the younger member of our group. Mikey wanted to see "Space Jams," yet again. But Meg and I wanted to see "Twister". Mr. Bennett thought "That Thing You Do" would be a good compromise. He opted to come along. In the end since both movies were playing simultaneously, He and his son went to see "Space Jams", and Meg and I got to see "Twister" which, we decided, wasn't all that scary. After the movies, Mr. Bennett suggested we stop and get some ice cream. When we got back to the house, I could tell my mom had been crying.

Grace Bennett and my mom were best friends after that.

Being an investment banker, Mom said I should save a full half of my pay in the bank and I could spend the other half. I knew she was right, so that's what I did. I didn't wear make-up or spend money on stupid stuff, like other kids my age. But I did want a double earphone jack so that when Meg and I were running we could both listen to the same songs on my Walkman. Mom said I should get a cell phone too so she could call me any time she needed.

Meg wanted a cell phone as well. When we got our first paychecks, Grace took us to Meijer where we picked out the best ones we could afford. Of course we both got the same one: a Nokia with a charging stand. That night I called Meg from my new cell phone. After that we were never out of contact.

Lance

All winter long, that first year we were in Michigan, Clyde and I ran together every day. It was his favorite part of the day, I could tell. He often wanted to stop and sniff something though, so I would let him. I would run in place while he did the sniffing and then start up again when he was ready to go again. Only occasionally did he yank me so hard that he jerked my arm, but I could handle it.

Not so with my poor mom.

Scott and I were at football practice that summer. He was on the varsity this year since it was his senior year. I was still on the J.V. squad. Mom called the school to pull him out of practice, telling the coach there was a family emergency. "This is all your fault, if I have to get in trouble with coach for leaving early, then so do you."

"What's wrong?" I asked him.

"It's your damn dog," he said.

Mom was sitting on the couch when we got home. She was holding her arm in a really weird way.

"What's wrong Mom?" I asked.

"Your dog got out again. He started tearing around the house and knocking things over. So I let him out in the yard. I got a soup bone to try and lure him into the kennel but he kept jumping at me and he grabbed hold of it. I tried to keep hold of it too but he yanked my arm so hard that I dislocated my shoulder. Then someone heard me crying in pain and opened the gate to see what was wrong with me. The dog bolted out of the yard. By that time I said forget it. I don't care, let the damn thing go."

"Mom," I said. "Which way did he go?"

She looked at me like I was insane, "I don't know," she said. "You boys have to take me to the hospital."

All at once, I was ashamed that I was thinking about my dog when my mom was sitting here injured. We got her into the car and I buckled her in.

Dad was at a Public Relations session at some high school in another state, so we couldn't reach him. Scott drove Mom to the hospital. I sat in the back seat, but I was looking everywhere for Clyde. I had no idea where he would have gone. I was heart sick. Nothing could have been worse than this.

They put big shots in my mom's shoulder to numb her arm up. Then the doctor pulled it back into place. It popped and she said it felt better, but the pop made me nauseous. Afterward, I couldn't stop telling mom how sorry I was.

"You better go try and find him," Mom told me. "I'll call the Humane Society and see if they picked him up or if anyone turned him in."

I went out to look for him, running through all our normal routes. I kept calling him and calling him. He was nowhere. It was my fault this happened. I should not have left him in my room when I left for school. From now on, I would make sure he spent the days out in the kennel. If I ever got him back that is.

Cathryn

By the end of that summer Mom was feeling a lot better. So was I. I had gotten my braces off, and had talked mom into letting me have contacts. Meg had grown to a whopping 5' 3", and had finally gotten her period. She was now a B cup and looked pretty nice in her new swim suit.

Shortly before school started Mom and I saw a Great Dane that seemed to be wandering around the Barton Hills neighborhood. We had never seen it before and it looked like it might be in trouble, so mom told me to get a leash out of the back of the car and we would see if we could capture it.

The thing stood chest high on me, and I'm not short. It would have towered over Meg. He was very definitely a male dog, and he was hungry. When we came upon him, he had just killed a rat. At least I hoped it was a rat and not a small dog, he was attempting to eat it raw but he didn't really like it.

"Did you miss your breakfast?" Mom asked the dog. It answered her with a loud single blurb of a bark. "I'm sorry to hear that. Come here boy, I'll see what we can do to get you some proper food! Come on, come here," she kept coaxing him with baby talk until finally he allowed her to pet him. "Now, that's a good boy. Now Bow, I want you to come and take hold of that leash handle, but don't put your hand through the loop just hold on to it tight." She was talking in the same tone of voice that she had been to the dog, so as to not spook him. But I knew what she was getting at. She knew he outweighed her, but the two of us together could secure him.

"There you are boy, what a good boy you are, yes," she told him. She had his face looking toward her and she was looking directly into his eyes, establishing dominance before she attached the leash. When she finally clicked on the leash, she anchored the leather strap by wrapping it once around her hand, and showed me to do the same. I was holding it with both hands. "He's going to yank us both," she told me.

"I know. He's a powerful dog." I said. I should have kept quite though because when I spoke he perked up his ears and decided to be elsewhere.

He stood and began to run. Mom and I ran with him for a short distance, but at the same time we were trying to control him by pulling on his leash. He was pulling so hard to get away from us that he was beginning to cut off his airway.

"Calmly, calmly," Mom said to him. "Stop!" she said sharply in a low tone. This was what I called her alpha dog voice. At once the dog stopped trying to run away and turned standing to look at her. When a dog turns like that, it's for one of two reasons and we didn't know which reason it was. Either he was turning because he recognized us as the alpha and was obeying us. Or he turned because he knew he was the alpha and he was about to subdue us. If that was the case we were in trouble, because he was a big powerful dog and Mom was sick. If she showed any sign of fear, he would attack.

She made a clicking noise with her tongue and followed it will the word, Heel! Again spoken sharply in a low tone. She clicked her tongue again, and showed him with her hand what she wanted him to do. She wanted him to come next to the two of us and sit down facing the same direction that we were facing. He looked at us as if we were some weird form of two headed monster, holding his leash in its four arms.

She repeated the command and then he got it. He calmly circled around to our right side and sat down on the sidewalk. Mom reached down and stroked him on the side of the head. “Good Dog,” she said simply.

“I’m going to start walking with my right leg, you have to dog my footsteps OK?” she told me.

“Yeah, I get it.” I said.

“Go then step, OK?”

“Yep.”

“Go,” she said. I stepped and my leg was exactly behind hers. The dog stood to walk along beside us. But when we kept walking our usual pace he began to trot and was getting ahead of us. Mom tugged on the leash just once and clicked her tongue. He at once got back in line with us staying at our heels. After a few yards walking at our pace, Mom told me she was going to stop. When she did the dog stayed standing and she told him to sit. He didn’t. She told him again, he would not. So I pushed down on his back end and he sat. Mom put a hand in front of his face and told him to stay. She then signaled for me to drop the leash and she walked out in front of the dog. Then she came and stood next to him again. She rubbed his head once and again called him a good dog.

“Take the leash again, Bow.” I did as she requested and we again began to walk. He walked fine with her, but at one point he got distracted by the scents on a tree and stopped to take a sniff. She clicked her tongue and sharply said, "Heel." He stopped what he was doing and came to walk beside her again.

We did this for several minutes, making sure the huge animal would follow our commands without yanking anyone down or injuring anyone. When Mom was convinced she could trust him, we walked him back to the car and got him inside.

We couldn't take him home because Mom hadn't been cleared to take rescue dogs yet after her illness. So we drove him to the shelter.

Rodney Blake was the director at the shelter. He was the local vet and handled all the new incoming cases. He was also the one that could clear mom to take in more rescued dogs.

"Hey, how have you been doing?" he asked mom.

"I'm getting there. Not quite ready yet, but getting there."

"How are you doing, Bow?"

"I'm good, but I'm going by Cathryn now."

"Oh, Cathryn? That's your real name?"

I chuckled and so did Mom. No one knew my real name.

"OK," he said. "Who is this?"

"No tags, but he looks to be pretty well fed. I am thinking he's lost. He had absolutely no training. We got him to stop, heel, sit and walk after working with him for about fifteen minutes, but this guy has been acting all alpha with whoever owns him. He's pretty dangerous."

"Did he bite you? Or growl?"

"No, he did turn on us though and if I wasn't showing dominance, I would have thought he might have attacked. Someone has let him think he's alpha dog for too long."

Rodney was looking the dog over, lifting his jowls to inspect his teeth. "He's only about four years old. So you've already proven he's trainable. If we find his owner I'm going to refer them to you for training. OK?"

"I'm not clear for rescue dogs, yet."

"You are the best trainer I have, so I want you to train these people. Can you do that?"

"Yes, I can." Mom said. She looked at me, as if asking if I would help. I smiled.

"I'll help," I said.

"You're a big help to your mom, aren't you?" Rodney asked me.

"I try to be."

"What grade are you in now?"

"I'm starting tenth this year."

"Ah, big sophomore!"

I smiled.

When we left the shelter, I said good-bye to the Great Dane and wondered if I would ever see him again.

“I hope he doesn’t go back to his original owners,” I told Mom. “They’ve had him for four years and never got him even the least amount of training. They can’t be that great.”

“Some people don’t want a trained dog, Bow. Even if it’s just house trained, that’s enough for some people.”

“This dog could injure people though. He’s got a mind of his own and if they don’t control him, he’ll end up controlling them.”

“I know, Bow.”

School was starting again soon and I was ready for it.

I was hoping that guy Scott had grown up a little since last year. He was a senior this year. I hoped he had forgotten about me over the summer.

The only thing that changed though was me.

My first day back at school I walked in with head held high. I looked so much better than before with my braces gone and now I had contacts. I had gone through a skin treatment regimen. Meg and I worked on that together. She and I both had clear skin, and good runner’s body’s now. So it was totally unfair that as soon as Meg and I got to our lockers, we heard that familiar voice. Lynn was coming down the hall toward us, her boyfriend Scott right beside her.

"Hey look, Scott, it's Bow Wow and Minnie Mouse."

But Scott was looking away. He didn't join in. No one else did either. I looked at them all straight in the face as they passed by us. There was one boy who I knew was in our grade. He looked right at me.

"Hi," he said.

"Hi," I said back. That was it. Then they all continued down to the jock hall where they hung out between classes.

"What is Lance doing saying hi to you?" Meg asked. "He's Scott's younger brother. Those are the astronaut's kids."

"Astronaut, really?"

"Yes, haven't you heard about them?" Meg asked.

"I guess not."

"Yeah, their father was one of the shuttle astronauts. I don't know which one. He's been in space though, someone said more than once. I don't know for sure. Anyway, there are five boys in the family. Steve is the oldest, he graduated last year. He plays football for Michigan State now. And then Scott is the next oldest. He's going to be the big football star this year everyone says. Then there's Lance. He plays football, basketball and runs track."

"I know, I saw him on the track team last year but I never talked to him."

"Probably wise. Then they have two younger brothers still. I'm telling you, it's a smorgasbord. They are all blond, they are all athletic, and their all freaking cute!"

"Meg. If they're all like Scott, then how can you possibly think they're cute? I thought you were the one who said that you see the inner beauty in people not the outward beauty."

"True, but outwardly they are all beautiful boys!!!"

"Stop," I said. "When did you see the younger ones?"

"At the final track meet last year. Their father was there too. He made quite a scene. Everybody thinks astronauts are interesting."

"Well, how about this," I said. "What if we go about our year without acknowledging that Scott and Lynn exist? We can just pretend they are blank space."

"OK, sounds like a good idea to me."

The year went rather well after that. My mom was in good spirits. She was in remission again. She held onto hope that this time it would hold for years. I kept asking if we could start to take in rescue dogs again, but she said she couldn't make that decision yet, not until she got her six month check-up. That happened in February of my sophomore year. She was all clear. So she informed me that next time a rescue took place, we would be able to take the dog or dogs in question.

"What about that Great Dane?" I asked mom. "Do you think we could get him back?"

"No, he's already gone. I don't know what happened to him. I think maybe they found his owner. I saw some posters up around the neighborhood after we found him. So I'm sure he got back home safely."

"But we're going to get a dog soon?" I asked.

"Well, let's not hope too soon," Mom said. I knew what she meant. Because they are rescue dogs we always hope that there won't be any. And yet, there always seem to be more coming in every month. In a perfect world, people like us wouldn't be needed at all.

Meg and I kept our jobs through the fall until the ice cream shop closed due to cold weather. Naomi asked us if we would consider working for her next year. She said she really enjoyed the two of us and hoped we would come back. She even promised us a raise.

Meg and I ran every day that we could. We lived about a mile away from each other. So every other day one of us would have an extra mile to run after school.

In March a new Subway shop opened a half mile from school so Meg and I decided to try it. We ran the half milc, sat and shared a Tuna sub—we both loved tuna—and afterward we ran back to school. It worked. It only took us 22 minutes to do that. We still had 8 minutes to get to class. We decided to do that every other day. By pooling our lunch money, we had enough to get a foot-long sub to share.

It was good too because a month later, when track training started, she and I were ready for it. All that good fish protein made us strong, and the thick bread gave us some stamina. Coach said we were the strongest girls on the team.

She and I had both gotten faster. We were dominating our team with speed and stamina both. I was allowed to run the mile and the 5K. Meg ran the 5K with me, but she wanted to run the 440 as well and see if she could win a ribbon. I was still the strongest runner for the 220, and my coach wanted to win, so she kept me on that race as well.

"Hey, Lance is looking at you," Meg told me one day at training.

"So?" I said.

"So, maybe he likes you."

"Again I say, so?"

"He's cute," Meg said.

"For a jerk!"

"How do you know he's a jerk?"

"Like brother like younger brother."

"Look at whose judging people by their close associates," she said.

That put me in my place. Not that it mattered. I wasn't interested.

"I'd rather have a dog, than a boyfriend."

"With him you could have both, he's got a dog."

"How do you know?"

"He goes out running with it every day. Thing is almost as tall as me. It could knock me down with its tail."

"I only saw one dog that big. It was a Great Dane. Mom found it wandering around the neighborhood last summer."

"Probably him. I know he was lost for a while last summer. They found him, got him back."

"Oh man," I said. I remembered thinking that I hoped his original owners didn't get him back because they probably didn't know how to treat him. It just gave me one more reason to not like that family.

Lance

It shouldn't have been any surprise to me, but in my sophomore year my brothers took over my life. Now, not only did I have a famous dad, but I had a famous brother who played for Michigan State, and more locally, my brother Scott was the big football star at our high school.

My next little brother was starting for the J.V. team. I sat on the bench on the Varsity team. Life just wasn't fair.

But it was even more unfair when my little freshman brother came home and announced that he and his girlfriend were going to the movies.

I didn't like any of my friends because they were still all hangers-on from people who liked the fact that my dad was an astronaut or they were friends who knew me because of my brothers. Every time I tried to make friends with someone I thought was cool, they would look at me like I was from Rigel 10 and got out of my way.

I couldn't even introduce myself to that tall girl. She was real pretty and a good runner. But I didn't know her name. My brother called her Bow Wow, the dog girl. I sure as heck wasn't going to ruin my chances with her by calling her that. I even tried to talk with her friend, that real short cute girl. But she just walked past me like I wasn't there.

I'd only ever said one word to her, "Hi." Yippee, I said hi to a girl!

In the spring of my sophomore year, I saw them leaving school in their running shoes during lunch. I wanted to follow them, but I didn't want to get caught. Two days later, they did it again.

It took me about three weeks to get up the courage to follow them. When I did I found that they were running to the Subway shop for lunch. I had skipped my own lunch to find this out. I didn't have enough money to buy a sub, nor could I eat one in the middle of a run. I didn't see how *they* could. I hid in the bushes when they came out and I followed them back to school.

I got so hungry that afternoon that I skipped my last class and went home to eat. I was just lucky that Mom wasn't home yet. I tried to take Clyde on a run after that, but I had to cut it short because of the undigested food in my stomach. I had no idea how those two girls could eat a six inch sub and then run back to school afterward. I couldn't do it.

I was really crushing on her. I was making myself miserable. So one night after track training, I followed her home. She and the short girl ran to a house about two miles from school. I don't know which of them lived there. I couldn't wait around to find out. The house they ran to was in the complete opposite direction to my house. I had followed them two miles and now I would have to run another five miles to get home to my house. I didn't have enough money to ride the bus. I needed to get home and feed Clyde, so I called my brother.

"What the hell, dude," my brother said to me when he picked me up at Wendy's about a mile away.

"Shut up," I explained.

"Seriously?"

But I was unresponsive after that, so he just shook his head and drove me home.

I wondered how long it would take me to get up to where I could run for six miles. Because that's how far I would have to run with Clyde in order to get into that girl's neighborhood. So I started. The first day I made it five miles. I went once through her neighborhood and then circled back to my house. Clyde was worn out that day. He went to my bedroom and lay on my bed for the rest of the night, not moving.

Cathryn

That summer before our junior year, two really great things happened. Meg and I had gotten a raise at the ice cream shop, and the Great Dane came back.

In August we were called in to help rescue a litter of newborn puppies that had been thrown into a garbage can within minutes after they were born. Every volunteer was called into the shelter to help care for them. The mother was also taken out of the home once they were found. A neighbor had called it in. The neighbor had heard them in the garbage can and checked it out. He had pulled five of them out of the can. Two were already dead by the time he found them.

He called the shelter and reported them, then he and his wife came in to help with the rescue effort. The mother dog, an abused golden retriever, was removed from the home along with the rest of the litter. They were undersized for newborn retriever pups, which indicated that the mother had been starved while she was pregnant.

There were fifteen tiny little pups. We fed them every half hour with an eye dropper.

Meg didn't want to leave the shelter at 10:00 P.M. when Jack and Grace came to get her, so they stayed and helped. The pups had to be kept warm, fed every time they woke which was about every twenty to thirty minutes, and even then some of them were not expected to live through the night. We hoped we had gotten them in time, but Mom said she had never seen a worse situation.

The mother dog was so malnourished and exhausted from her labor that she had to be hand fed and was receiving I.V. fluids. Over the course of the night, despite our best efforts three more of the pups died.

At 6:00 A.M. more volunteers came in to help and Rodney told me, Mom, Meg and her parents to go home and get some rest. We all agreed to come back in at 4:00 P.M. to relieve the volunteers.

Meg and I had a shift at the ice cream shop the next day, but when we told Naomi what we had been doing, she told us to stay home and get some rest. We went back the next day, but the number of pups dwindled to ten and then to seven.

Out of 17 pups, only six survived past the first week. It was heart breaking. I asked Mom if we could adopt one of them.

"We're on the list," she said. "Everyone wants one of them. There won't be enough to go around."

I nodded. The six pups would have good forever homes. I hoped we would win the lottery in four or five months when they were able to be adopted.

But I couldn't leave it alone. I called the shelter every day to find out how they were doing. Rodney told me again and again that they were doing fine, they were thriving. I kept asking, "Is there anything I can do? Just ask, please, anything!"

"It's all taken care of. There isn't anything more any of us can do that isn't already being handled."

After a couple weeks of this, Rodney called my mother to ask her if I needed something to do to keep my mind off the pups. So together they got me another job. I started walking the dogs at the shelter. It fit in perfectly with my ice cream shop job. Of course it was just volunteer work. But then, when I was at the dog park with four of the dogs from the shelter, a man came up to me.

"How much do you charge to walk dogs?"

I had no idea how to answer that, so I said, "It depends."

"On what?"

"On lots of things, on how big the dog is, how difficult it is to train him on the leash, how far he can go, if he plays nice with others, lots of things."

"OK, well where do you start?"

"Have you ever had a dog walker before?"

"No, I just got this dog, and I'm finding that she needs more attention than I can give her any one day."

"Where do you live?"

He lived in my neighborhood about seven blocks from me. I could easily pick up his dog on my way to getting the shelter dogs. I had him call his girl over and introduce her to me. She was a very enthusiastic springer spaniel about two years old.

I put her on her leash and told her to heel. She didn't know what I meant. So I showed her what I meant. I stepped out in front of her and told her to heel. She didn't do it. So I told her to sit. She sat. She knew that one. Then I told her to heel again, and showed her what was expected once more. She did it and I praised her up and down. I tried walking with her and kept telling her to heel. Then I stopped and she sat right away. She was a smart dog.

Then I called over one of my shelter dogs, a fox terrier mix and put him on a leash. I told them both to heel. It took a second, but they lined up next to my leg. The Springer sniffed the smaller dog once or twice but when I started walking, they both heeled quickly following my lead.

When I came back to the man I said, "She's a smart one, and she plays well with others. OK, ten dollars a week for walking, and I don't do weekends. You don't work on weekends do you?"

"No, I have every weekend off."

"OK, then you walk her on the weekends. I'll build up her stamina so she can walk up to about 5 miles. I don't just walk them, I sometimes run with them. So she might be a little tired the first few days until she gets into shape."

"How much for the training?" he asked.

"For the training, well, I'll train her while I walk her. But for you it's a one-time fee of $30. I'll come to your home and train you and your whole family so that she will know what to expect of you."

"You'll train her for free, but it'll cost me $30 to train me and my wife?"

"Yep," I said. "This girl is a natural, it's people that need to be trained." I smiled at him. He agreed offering me his handshake. He gave me his card and we made arrangements on when and where I could pick up his dog in the mornings. Then we made an appointment for me to come over on Saturday so I could train him and his wife. It was the easiest $40 I ever made in one week.

After that, word of mouth started getting around. Soon I had more calls for dog walking. I catered to the clientele who were young married couples, who both worked full time jobs, and who considered their dog as their baby with obvious exceptions. I doubted even these people would leave a baby home alone for 10 hours while they went to work. And if their baby got leukemia they would fight with every dime they had. But if the dog got leukemia, it would be a quick euthanasia.

I really have no right to complain though, because within weeks I was making an average of $100 a week or more depending on the dogs. I found that eventually I had to break them up into two groups, each got individual attention that way while we were at the dog park, and even though their walks were shorter, they were still getting plenty of exercise because I was running with the larger ones and walking fast with the smaller ones. Plus I made an extra $30 for each new dog I picked up because I had the training exercise with the dog parents.

No one thought I was taking advantage of them and they all were really bummed out when I said I had to cut back because of my school schedule. I stopped walking the shelter dogs when school started and after school I walked the clients' dogs. It still worked out great.

Late in August, Mom got a call from Rodney at the clinic. The Great Dane owner had contacted the shelter and wanted a referral for a dog trainer. Mom said yes at once. We sat down to discuss how this was going to work.

"You are going to have to be the hands on trainer," Mom told me. "The doctor said that the radiation would cause my bones to become brittle and fragile, I don't want to take any chances."

"Is it wise to take on this dog at all?" I asked her.

"Well, I said yes because I know how strongly you felt about him. Do you want to give him a pass?"

"No, I want to train him. I think he's trainable."

His name was Clyde, and his owner was a pretty woman by the name of Elaine Devers. She said that her son was the actual owner, but he was off at football camp for a couple of weeks before school started up again.

"You must know my son, Lance, he's in your grade."

"Oh, yes? He's on the football team?"

"Yes, and he plays basketball and runs track."

"I should know him then since I run track too."

"I know, you are quite a talented runner. But that's why Lance wanted this dog. He wanted a dog he could run with."

"I should really be training him," I told her.

"Yes, I know, but he doesn't really have a problem with the dog, I do. I want to be able to control him."

I liked her. I had to train her how to be the alpha dog in the family, she was too timid around him and he knew how to get his way with her. Together, she and I became a united front and the dog didn't stand a chance. He became the follower.

Mrs. Devers smiled the first time she gave him a command and he followed it. She stood a little straighter after that.

We trained him to sit whenever he started to act like he wanted to jump up on someone. She gave him a huge floor pillow for a bed and we trained him to "go lay down," on it. She taught him to stay. I taught him to heel and to behave on a leash. He already knew how to run with someone on the leash but there was a problem with that. He would stop at any pole, building, fire hydrant, tree and fence and sniff to see who had been there before him. I thought this was a bad habit that Lance had allowed to perpetuate.

But when WE ran, I was the alpha dog, not him. If I didn't want to stop, he wasn't allowed to stop. So I trained him with a tug on his collar to not stop while I was running.

Every time I could see that he wanted to stop, I would give him another nudge and keep him from getting distracted.

Later, I described this behavior to Mrs. Devers. “Every time the dog stops and your son allows it, he is letting Clyde be the dominant dog, and it’s a mixed signal. Clyde can never be top dog, he has to be controlled. So, you need to tell your son to jerk his chain when he gets distracted and not allow him to stop until he is ready to stop.”

“I will tell him that.”

Mrs. Devers was a good student. When she was finished with our training session, she was in control. Clyde was a great dog. He was so well behaved. It was almost as if he was happy that someone was curbing his bad behavior. He truly loved being the “Good Boy.”

“I’m kind of sorry we won’t be seeing her again,” Mom told me. “I really liked her. We could be good friends.”

Lance

Last year, my brothers took over my life. This year my friends did.

The problem was that I didn't like most of my friends. I wished I could have hung around with the science geeks in the computer lounge. I wished I could have an intelligent discussion about quarks, and space, and worm holes. But I was a jock and I would be a jock until I graduated. It would only be a year from next June, but I could hardly wait. I planned to remake myself entirely in college.

My brothers had made sure everyone accepted me as a jock and because of that I couldn't associate with any other person, no matter how cool I thought it might be to have a friend who could beat me at chess, or who knew about the drive system on the Enterprise-D. I wanted to learn how to speak Kingon. And I wanted to read Orson Scott

Card during my lunch hour instead of torture people in the cafeteria.

I hated my friends. They were bullies. They thought they were entitled to treat people like trash. Just like my older brother who tortured people the entire two years he was here. He made up unfortunate nick-names. He constantly pointed out a weakness that a person exhibited one time and was never allowed to forget.

I tried to talk sense to these so-called friends. I said, "Leave him alone," more times than I can count. I tried to make things better for the kids who were the object of their torture.

But in the end I was weak. I didn't want to be on the other side of their wrath. So I kept my friends and only made token efforts to stand up against them. Of course, my most shameful moment was when I stopped one of my friends from beating a kid to death.

It was the night of the pep rally for the final game of the season. We were playing our cross-town rivals and feeling was high. Our captain, Jerry Smith, known by the team as Schmitty, had a true and bold hatred for this kid on the track team.

He was a little kid, by the name of Tony. He was 5' 4" and weighed about 120 pounds. He was a total ginger, and when he ran too long in the sun, his skin turned bright a red like a sun set. He had more pimples on his face than anyone I'd ever seen. But he could do the 440 in 55.24 seconds. And he held the school record for pole vaulting 18 feet 1 1/2 inches.

I don't know why Schmitty hated the guy. But he did. I don't know what the kid did to make Schmitty hate him so much, maybe he flipped Schmitty off. I don't know what happened. But I do know that after the rally, Schmitty and three other seniors trapped the kid in the back stair well and started taunting him.

I got there just as the altercation got violent. The kid tried to fight back, but it was four against one. I shamed the other three football players by telling them to stay out of it. "Let Schmitty fight his own battles." They stood back looking at me. I let Schmitty get a couple more punches in but then he gave him a jab, and I heard the bones in his nose crunch sickeningly. Schmitty then delivered an uppercut that floored the kid. His face was a bloody mess.

Schmitty got down on one knee over the kid and grabbed him by the shirt. He started pounding on the kid like he wanted him dead.

That's when I stepped in. I pulled Schmitty's jacket and threw him over toward our team mates.

"Hold him," I yelled at them. Two of the other guys grabbed him and held him back. I stood between him and the kid and just started repeating, "It's over. Come on, It's not worth it."

Finally Schmitty came to his senses, spat on the floor at my feet and walked off, his three friends behind him.

"You OK?" I asked the kid.

"Yeah," he said, as he tried to get up. I could tell the kid was far from OK. "Thanks," he said in a grudging voice.

"Let me help you get home." The kid stood, he leaned against the wall while he got his balance and then looked at me with utter hatred in his eyes.

"I'm not going home."

"Come on, let me help you. You can barely stand up."

"If I go home, my mother will press charges. I can't go home tonight."

"Where you going?"

"Believe it or not, I got friends."

"Those guys aren't my friends," I told him.

"Could have fooled me."

In the end he got his equilibrium and staggered out of the back door of the stair well. Last time I saw him that night, he was trudging across the field toward the parking lot.

I don't know what happened to him that night. But he was back at school on Monday with two big shiners. He was telling people he was in car accident.

"Yeah," Schmitty said. "His car ran into my fist."

I pulled Schmitty aside and said, "You want to go to jail? You almost killed that kid. All he had to do was tell people what really happened and you'd be locked up right now. You can't just go around beating on kids, you asshole."

"Yeah," he said to me, "You want some of this too?"

I just shook my head like I felt sorry for him. "Man, I don't know what you think you have to prove or to whom, but I don't need to help you prove it." I walked away from him and I never spoke to him again. He graduated in June and I never had to see him again.

But I was so ashamed of myself for not pulling him off the kid sooner.

In retrospect, this is the moment I decided to get rid of all the friends I hated and start to find friends that I actually liked.

Cathryn

Dog walking was becoming so lucrative for me that when summer came, I didn't bother going back to the ice cream shop with Meg. Meg and I still spent lots of time together. I found out that I had gotten into both Michigan State and Eastern Michigan University. Eastern was my safety school. I was still waiting though to find out if I had been accepted to Michigan. I still didn't know what I wanted to do. I guess I was leaning toward nursing. I thought maybe medical knowledge would be able to advance my career as a dog trainer better than anything else.

After track season was over, I increased my dog walking clientele to double. I was consistently making between $200 and $250 per week. I bought my own class ring, and my own senior pictures. I bought my year book, but I refrained from buying a lot of announcements. I figured there were only four people who needed to know about it other than Mom and Meg.

Meg had more friends than me. She was funny and gregarious, so she naturally attracted people. Half way through the summer she got a boyfriend too. His name was Tony McLeod. She had gotten to know him on the track team. He was a red-headed kid that was kind of accident prone. He was really fast. He ran the 440 in 55.24 seconds, and he held the school record for pole vault 18 feet 1 1/2 inches.

What was more important, he was short, but she was shorter. They seemed to be a match made in high school paradise. They were such a cute couple.

I was afraid, after they got together, that she wouldn't want to hang out with me anymore. But she did. She would tell him, "Go find some friends your own gender, I have to hang with my girlfriend!"

Our time together became quality time, more than quantity time, that summer. She took on more hours at the ice cream shop, nearly 40 hours a week, sometimes 50 if she took shifts for others on the weekends.

"I don't mind," she told me. "It's an easy job and I get all my meals."

Meg didn't like walking dogs so she would hang with Tony until I was finished. There were times when I wanted to go to a movie with her and she asked if it was OK if Tony came too. Her parents loved this. Grace took me aside one time and thanked me for chaperoning.

Meg and Tony were both 17 years old, but it didn't mean they were going to have sex. Meg told me she didn't like him that much. But it turns out that she was wrong. I'm quite sure she liked him that much. I don't know for sure if they did it. She wouldn't tell me. She said it was none of my business the one and only time I asked her. Tony was even more tight-lipped.

In October, I found out I was accepted to Michigan. That was my dream school! I really wanted to go there. I wanted to stay with my Mom. She was still in remission and I thought that if I got my nursing degree I could help her if she got sick again. Plus, I could keep all my clients and continue to walk dogs as my part time job while taking classes.

But shortly after I started making plans to go to Michigan, Mom canceled cable.

"Why?" I asked.

"Because I never watch it anymore and you never did. It's a waste of money."

She was right, I usually preferred to read or study. That had always been my habit while in school.

"What are you saving your money for?" I asked her.

"For school of course. Michigan is going to be expensive."

"Do you want me to go to Eastern?" I asked.

"No, I don't. I want you to have the opportunities that a big school will undoubtedly give you. Just keep your eyes and ears open and always say yes!"

"Always say yes?" I asked. I could think of a few questions off the top of my head that I might be asked in college to which the answer would logically be *NO*.

"When it comes to directions your life might take, or opportunities that might come your way, always say *YES*."

"But don't get pregnant too soon," I suggested this as a compromise.

"Honey, get pregnant whenever you please, but be sure it's your choice to be pregnant, and not something that just happened by accident."

"That's really all you're going to say to me about that?"

"You know my feelings on this topic. We talked about it when you went through puberty. You have all the information and if you don't, I'm absolutely sure you know where to find it."

"Yes, mom, I do."

"Oh, and while I have your attention, I called Rodney. I'm taking myself off the list for rescuing again."

"So you're just going to get rid of Friskey and then no more dogs again?"

"No, I'm keeping Friskey." Friskey was a Sheltie/Fox Terrier mix with cute floppy ears and a pretty brown coat. He stood about knee high on me and was one of the most exuberant and smart dogs we've ever had. We both loved him. I was glad that he would be around because he was the perfect companion dog for us both.

But that brought up another issue. I decided to address it straight forward.

"Mom, you're sick again aren't you?" I asked her point blank.

"I never could hide anything from you."

So now I only had one question for her. "Mom, you said you wanted to see me graduate, should I graduate in January?"

"No, I'll survive until June. Don't you worry about that. I couldn't have asked for a better daughter."

I started to cry and went to her. I sat down next to her on the couch and put my head on her lap. "Mom, why didn't you tell me?"

"There was no use. I knew you would figure it out sooner or later. Honey, I can't fight anymore. I'm tired. If it weren't for you, I wouldn't have lasted this long."

"Mommy," I said. I felt like a little girl again. "What am I going to do without you? You are the only steady thing in my life."

"That's so not true. In fact it's quite the opposite. I've been up and down so many times. I could always count on you. You're my rock. You're the one that can be counted on. Not me. You have always been the steadfast one in this relationship. That won't change when I'm gone."

"But Mom, I'm not old enough to be on my own. I've never even paid the bills."

"Well, let's talk about this then. Go get them."

I stood and went to the cupboard where my mom kept her checkbook and all the bills. She had written out a schedule of everything that needed to be paid and when. Amounts had been written in and everything was right there clearly denoted. The insurance on the house was paid, also on the car. She showed me where she kept the title for the car and said that next month on my birthday she would take me over to the Secretary of State and get it put in my name. I would get my permanent license the same day.

The house was paid for and she had put the deed in my name. Our health insurance was paid up until next year. She had just canceled the cable. The gas bill, power bill, trash pickup all had to be paid at the beginning of the month, and we were within easy running distance of each. She said that she tried to only use the credit card for emergencies and paid it off right away with her disability check.

She had put my name on her credit card so I could use it too. I didn't eat much, mostly salads and sometimes I splurged and bought pizza. Mom had ten ways to cook boneless skinless chicken breasts and that's what we had every night for supper. Grocery shopping for the two of us was simple. I had been handling that for over a year already.

I paid for my own phone service and dog supplies, which consisted of plastic bags to pick up poop, and healthy dog treats in three sizes.

She had a 401K pension from her former job at the bank, and she told me that she had arranged with her loan officer to transfer that money to a trust fund for me to live off of.

She said that I would get death benefits from Social Security after she died, all I had to do was apply and those would keep me in the house until I graduated from nursing school. I could keep going to school to get a four year degree if I wished and they would keep sending me death benefits as long as I stayed in school until I was 22.

She said I would also have the life insurance money, since she had whole life insurance that would pay off big time when she died. She had it all planned out. The trust fund would cover college expenses, but there was only a few thousand dollars in it right now. When I got the payout from the life insurance, I was to add it to the trust fund and ask my officer for an allowance that I thought I could live with.

Mom even had her funeral arrangements made and paid for. She was going to be cremated and she wanted me to spread her ashes in the cemetery over her parents' graves. She didn't want a memorial service, she only had three friends and they would show up and help me get things settled but only if I wanted them to. I asked her who they were.

"Meg's parents and Mrs. Devers."

"Those are your friends?" That surprised me.

"Honey, I never wanted to tell you this. But I lost track of my friends years ago. Your father took me away from everyone and everything that I loved. Then when I got sick, he couldn't hack it so he left too. I've been alone with no one but you. He wouldn't even let me go to my own father's funeral. I had co-workers over the years, and I had bosses, and I had volunteer coordinators, and vets, but no friends. Not until Meg's parents showed an interest. Then when I rescued Clyde we got to know his mother. Elaine called me a lot afterward wondering how I've been. She's been a good friend. But I think she hasn't had a lot of friends either since she moved here. Her husband was an astronaut you know."

"Yeah, I know," I said.

"You ran track with her son, Lance," Mom said.

I remembered my freshman year, and the stupid boy Scott who always called me Bow Wow. I remembered a younger version of him saying Hi to me and I ignored him. I remembered Meg telling me that Lance Devers was staring at me in practice. She had told me once that she had seen him with his dog running. I remember that pep rally when Tony got beat up. How Lance and four other guys had followed him down the stairs. But later I saw Tony talking with Lance in the hall. They seemed to be friends after that.

"Clyde belongs to Lance Devers?" I asked.

"Yes," Mom said. "Elaine tells me that Lance is going to Michigan next year."

I wanted to say, "So what?" But I didn't, because all at once I did care. I cared a lot. Maybe Lance wasn't the clone of his older—stupider—brother.

I looked down at the bills again, trying like crazy to come up with some other subject to talk about. "Are you sure there will be enough money? Maybe Meg can live with me, pay rent to help with the bills."

"If she wants to she can. Grace tells me she is going to Community College for the first two years. You two would make fine roommates. But if Tony wants to room with you too, you be sure and charge him as well."

I laughed. I couldn't imagine the three of us living in the same house. How long would it take before Meg moved into his room? Or would it be that way from the start? It was a bitter laugh, but at least I was laughing.

Once I made the connection between Lance Devers and Clyde, I began seeing them everywhere: the dog park, running in the Barton Hills neighborhood, even sometimes running in my neighborhood. I started saying hi to him when I saw him, as we ran past each other. Then one day in early April, about four days before my birthday I saw him at the dog park. Clyde was running around with no leash catching a Frisbee in his massive jaws. I let the six dogs that I was currently walking off their leashes so they could run and play and I walked up to him. Before I introduced myself I said, "Hey Clyde, hey buddy!"

Clyde came bounding up to me like he was going to knock me over and at the same time Lance and I both said, "Sit, Clyde." Clyde sat at my feet and I reached over to pat his head which stood hip high on me.

"Good Boy, who's a good boy, that's right, you're a good boy!"

Lance was laughing. "You're the one that trained him," he accused.

"Guilty," I said. He laughed again.

"You know, my mom took your lesson to heart. She tells us all now that she's the alpha dog and we are all lesser dogs. She rules our family the way you taught her to rule over Clyde." He was laughing again. I smiled.

"Good," I said.

Lance threw the Frisbee again and Clyde jumped back to fetch it.

"Well, I'd love to stand and chat but I got a job to do." I turned and called one of my dogs to me. She came running. I put her on the leash and began to put her through her paces.

When she had exhibited each behavior spot on perfect, I let her off the leash again and called to the next one. I tried really hard not to notice, but Lance was watching me. He looked like he wanted to ask me something but he didn't know how to start. I should have just asked him what he wanted to know. Then he would blurt out some awkward question and then afterward we could laugh about it. But all of a sudden, I didn't think it was my job to make his life easier. After all, my life is hard. My mom was dying. My dad was a deadbeat with another family. I was running my own business, and soon enough I wouldn't even have a family other than Friskey.

Lance had both parents, and they were alive, healthy, and still in his life. I had a job, and I had to pay for college myself. For all I knew the United States government was paying for his college, since he was the son of a NASA astronaut. His life was peachy next to mine. Why should I go out of my way for him?

I kept training my charges and putting them through their paces one by one. When finally I looked up from finishing with the fourth one, Lance and Clyde had gone.

“No guts, no glory,” I said to the little Jack Russell Terrier I was training. He cocked his head and looked at me trying to figure out what I wanted him to do with that statement. I just petted him and told him he was a good boy.

Lance

I hate my life. I hate my friends, all except for one. I made friends with Tony McLeod, the kid that Schmitty beat up last semester. I told him I was sorry. I should have stepped in sooner. I told him that if he wanted to press charges, I would tell them what I saw. I almost had two friends I liked. Only I didn't know her name. I thought about asking her name, but I didn't.

Instead I came home and asked my mom what her name was.

"I saw that girl that trained Clyde in the dog park," I told my mom.

"Oh, Bow?" mom said.

"Bow? That's her name?"

"Yes, B-O-W, Bow. It's a nickname I think. I don't know her real name. Her mother called her Bow."

"Scott used to call her Bow Wow."

"Yeah, well, maybe when he gets to be thirty he'll grow up finally."

My mother had no motherly illusions about how imperfect her sons were. She knew us all right down to our teeth. She knew that Steve was the oldest and the more arrogant. She knew that Scott always tried to measure up to both Steve and Dad and could never quite make it so he over compensated by trying to make other people look bad. She knew that I was shy and withdrawn, and a total follower. She knew that Michael was a player, always seeking attention and playing the shock and awe card. And she knew Paul was the scamp, the little sweetheart with the mean streak who could make you laugh as fast as he could break your heart.

Mom also knew that I tried to be a stand-up guy. But it didn't always work. I was too much of a coward.

"Why don't you just ask her?" Mom suggested. "Just man up and ask her name. She'll respect you for it."

"Mom, I can't do that, I've been going to school with her for almost four years now. I should know her name."

"Why are you in such a quandary over this? Do you like her?"

"Mom," I whined.

"It's OK, you're a senior. It's time you got yourself a girlfriend. Heck, Paul already has a girlfriend."

Paul was a freshman this year. He did indeed have a girlfriend, and she had already been over to meet them all. But for some strange reason, I didn't think she would last.

"I don't . . ." I sighed. It was useless to finish this sentence, because Mom already knew it was a lie.

"It's alright. You don't have talk to her now, while you're still both in high school. She's going to Michigan next year."

"Oh, Mom," I said, and I couldn't keep the pain from my voice. I knew now that she would be in school with me for the next four years as well. I had a science scholarship to Michigan. I was going to start out in the Physics department and maybe go into Astrophysics. If NASA ever got the space race going again, I was going to be one of the first to go to Mars. I would be ready at least. Or I would end up as a high school Physics teacher. But whatever. Life is full of disappointments.

I couldn't help myself. A couple of days later I went back to the dog park. It was after school and I knew she would be there training. So I thought I'd casually run into her again. But I was surprised. When I got there, Tony and his girlfriend were there. There was an old lady in a wheel chair sitting next to a card table. There was a cake on the card table. A bunch of other people who all had leashes stood around the table too. When

Tony saw me he waved me over. I let Clyde off the leash and went over to say hi.

"Lance, just in time for some cake, bro. It's Cathryn's birthday."

"I thought your girlfriend's name was Meg."

"My girlfriend," pulling her toward him, "This is Meg, my girlfriend. That is Cathryn, Meg's best friend. But you know her. We're all on the same track team!"

"Hi Cathryn," I said. She looked at me funny.

"Hi, Lance," she said. But she hesitated over the name a little like it was a word from a foreign language.

"Happy Birthday."

"Thanks." She went back to talking with one of the adults that was carrying a leash.

"Never mind her," Meg said. "Her mom invited all of her clients here for cake. These were just the ones that could make it. Cathryn's best friends besides me are her dogs."

"I know, she trained Clyde," I admitted. "My mom couldn't handle him. He's too big, too much dog."

Meg smiled at me and then looked at Tony significantly. Tony scowled and then turned to me again. He pulled me off a little so his words could not be overheard.

"I just asked Meg to go to Prom with me. But she doesn't want to go without Cathryn.

And Cathryn doesn't have a date, so Meg is saying she wants to go stag with her. She tells me that if I want to go to prom with her, then I should find Cathryn a date too. So what to do you say? Help a guy out? You don't have a date yet do you?"

"No, but," I said.

"I know, she's tall, and she usually smells like dog shit, but that's because she carries it around with her. I'm sure she won't take any to prom."

"That's not it . . ." I said, but I couldn't go any further.

"Then what?" he asked.

I was a total loss. I didn't know what to say. He had taken me by surprise. If I had been ready for this I would have said, yeah man set me up. I'll go. I'll help you out dude, not a problem. But I was hesitating. Why? Because I wanted to go to Prom with her. I wanted to make sure she knew it wasn't a set up. I wanted to ask her, I wanted to plan it. Take her out to dinner beforehand, I wanted to make it the most perfect prom date anyone ever had for both me and her. I liked her. It was just as my mom had said. I'd been looking for her. I wanted to run with her. I had wanted to train with her. I wanted to talk with her about how she trained Clyde. I wanted to help her walk the dogs. I wanted to do everything with her.

"I don't think she likes me," I said. But even to my ears it sounded lame.

We were interrupted when she called out to Clyde.

"Here Clyde, Here boy."

I couldn't help myself. I smiled. She was down on one knee and was letting him lick her face. He nearly knocked her down, and then he did. She fell on her butt laughing. I couldn't help myself I laughed too. She pulled him down on top of her. He was still licking her chin. She was tucking in her lips and biting them closed so that he wouldn't be able to lick the inside of her mouth. But then he started licking her nose. She pushed him off and sat up telling him to sit. He stopped licking her when he heard the command. She was alpha once again.

"Ugh, you were going to drown me in spit," she said. All of a sudden I didn't think it was funny anymore.

"Lay down, Clyde," I said, maybe a little too sternly. He followed my command at once. "Let me help you, Bow Wow," I said. Then all at once I realized what I had done. She glared up at me and did not take my offered hand.

I didn't know how to correct this mistake, how to unsay it. I had no way to tell her how sorry I was. But I had to try.

"Cathryn, I mean, Cathryn. I know your name. I'm so . . ." I choked. "I didn't mean to . . ."

"Thanks," she said abruptly. "For bringing Clyde, you know how much I love him. I'm really glad he's here at my birthday party."

As she walked away from me I felt miserable. I wanted to hide. The old woman in the wheel chair sliced the cake and served up the pieces onto paper plates. It was not chocolate cake I noticed. So it was OK if one of the dogs licked the plate. Meg brought two pieces of cake over to where I was standing, away from the others. Tony was following her with another piece. The three of us stood there and silently ate cake.

"She knows you didn't mean it in a nasty way," Meg said to me. "She knows you're not the same as your brother."

"Still, I should not have called her that."

"No, but I think she'll get over it. You're still going ask her to the prom aren't you?" Meg asked me.

"I didn't think she liked me before, she must hate me now."

"She can't hate you. She likes your dog. Besides she doesn't have enough energy to waste on hating someone."

"What's that mean?" I asked.

"Her mother is dying, she doesn't have anyone else. She's just sad, not hateful."

I couldn't believe it. I looked at the old woman in the wheelchair maybe for the first time. She wasn't old at all. She was my mom's age. She was wearing a head scarf and a shawl to keep her warm in the April coolness. She had a blanket over her lap. She had bags under her eyes and she was wearing a forced bright smile. She was trying to put on a good face, but really this was an ordeal for her. I could feel the water coming into my eyes. I sniffed. I didn't want to cry in front of everyone. I handed Meg my plate and called Clyde over. I blinked back tears as I got him on the leash and then I ran. I ran all the way home.

Mom was in the kitchen when I got there. She had Clyde's meal cooling in the steel bowl. I tested it and put him in the kennel to wait for it

"What's the matter with you," Mom asked.

"Cathryn's mother is dying," I said.

"Denise, yes, she is. She has been ill since Bow was in second grade. She's losing the battle."

"Mom," I said but I couldn't go on. My voice cracked. I ran up to my room and lay on my bed sobbing. I didn't even know why at the time. I didn't feel sorry for myself, or for her, or for her mother. Well I did feel sorry for both her and her mother but that's not why I was crying. I was crying because I was so weak, and she was so strong. I had everything. I had two parents who lived together in the same house, who loved me. I had other siblings that made my life unbearable most of the time but in truth I knew I could count on them. I had no worries. I had nothing to rightly complain about. I had everything and still I hated my life. She had nothing, and soon she would have even less, but she was rock steady and calm and still she could shame me with one look. Why did I call her that? Why would I have made that mistake? I felt like the worse person on the planet. She deserved someone so much better than me.

Cathryn

Mom and I agreed—no tears. We both expected this, and we both knew it was coming. She said she wanted me to be happy in the end. She wanted to go out looking at my smiling face.

I did my fair share of crying during the months of April and May. But I hid it. I didn't want mom to know I was crying. I only cried once in front of someone—Meg—and it helped. I knew that Mom wanted me to be strong. But I could only be strong with her. I knew I would have to cry myself out at some point. But it would not be in front of my Mom.

Meg came over nearly every night. Tony was at our house most nights as well. Sometimes Meg would call her parents and tell them that no one was in the mood to cook. Grace would either come over and cook for all of us, or she and Jack would come over together with take out.

"You guys," Mom said the night they brought over about $100 worth of Chinese food from Mom's favorite restaurant. "You are going to make sure I have all of my favorite dishes, aren't you?"

By this time no one disputed the fact that my mom was going to die. She didn't try to sugar coat it. I was 18 now and she treated me like an adult. She knew that Grace and Jack Bennett would be there for me, if I needed them. I was going to try not to need their help, but it was good to know I had it all the same.

After dinner Meg and Tony started talking about the prom again.

"Do you have a date yet, Cathryn?" Grace asked.

"We thought we had date for her, but he said he didn't think she liked him," Tony said.

"Translation," I said, "He didn't like me."

"I think he does like you though," Meg said. "Tony, didn't you say you thought he liked Cathryn?"

"Yeah, he likes you alright. He always asks about you."

"Who Lance?"

"Yeah, Lance," Tony said. "He was embarrassed because he called you that name."

"Yeah and what about that?" I asked. "Where does he get off? If he's trying to get on my good side, he shouldn't be using the name the bullies gave me. That is not a good move."

"What did they call you?" Jack asked out of curiosity.

"Bow Wow the dog girl," I said.

He cleared his throat and I could see him trying not to laugh. Meg laughed at her father's attempts not to laugh. Then Tony laughed at Meg and then we were all laughing. Even Mom.

"Well, you are a dog trainer," Jack said.

"True, but they were really mean about it."

"Maybe you ought to take it back," Tony said.

"What do you mean?" I asked.

"You know, maybe you ought to embrace it."

"Do you know how the River Rats got their name?" Jack asked the group at large.

"Are we about to get an ancient history lesson?" Meg asked her father.

"Quiet you," he said. "No really? Do you know?"

"OK," I said. "Tell me how the River Rat became our mascot."

Jack began his story. "It was back a couple of years before I went there. There was only one high school in Ann Arbor, Pioneer High. While the new school was being built they had to house both sets of students in the one existing high school. Two different entities under the same roof. Two different sets of teachers, two different sets of curriculum, even two different sets of sports teams. That way, when the new school was ready half way through the semester they could just shift to the new building and keep everything else intact. So while they were in the old school together, the Pioneers began to call the Huron High students the River Rats, because their new school was next to the Huron River."

I nodded. I thought I could see where this story was going. "So when it came time to choose a mascot, they picked the River Rats?"

"They had other suggestions. They thought about having tigers, and wolverines, and grizzlies and things like that. River Rats wasn't even on the list when they voted. So the students did a write-in vote and an overwhelming majority wanted to be known as the River Rats. Well, the administration thought it was totally inappropriate so they decided to have the vote again with a few different nominations. The Lions, the Badgers, etc. But when it came time for the vote, they again did a write in and River Rats again won by a landslide. So this time the principal said, 'OK, you all want to be known as the River Rats? You got it! We're the River Rats!"

"It became a source of pride," Tony said.

"So you think I should call my business Bow Wow Dog Walking and Training Service, run by Bow Wow the Dog Girl?"

"That would sure show those bullies, now, wouldn't it?" Jack asked me.

"I have to admit, it's a good idea. Especially when you consider how I got that name in the first place." I recounted how my teacher had written Wow! Under my name on a test before she handed it back. That dweeb on the J.V. team had seen it because he was sitting in front of me. The only reason she wrote it on there was because I'd aced the test and even answered the extra bonus question to give myself an A+. I was the only one in the class that did that, so I deserved the Wow!

"Maybe he called me that because he knew I was smarter than him," I said half to myself.

Mom nodded. Mom always let me make my own discoveries.

"I'll get you some cards printed up," Mom said.

"You are going to Prom though," Grace said to me like it was a forgone conclusion.

"I don't think so. It's the day before graduation and I just think I'll stay home with mom."

"No, you have to go to your prom. You are going to hate yourself if you miss it," Mom said. "Besides, if you don't go, what am I going to do with that dress I bought you?"

"You did not!"

"Yes, she did." Grace said. "She came with us when Meg picked out hers."

Meg nudged me. "You were too busy remember. You had a training session with those yuppies down the block."

"I remember," I turned toward mom, "but I didn't know you had gone too."

"Surprise!" Mom said smiling.

"I've always wanted to show up with two women on my arms," Tony said.

"Oh, Pig," Meg exclaimed swatting him on the shoulder.

"Oww!"

"So, you'll go right?" Mom persisted.

"I suppose," I said.

"Good," Meg told me. "I already bought your ticket."

The night of the prom though, I got another surprise. Meg and her mom came over to my house so they could help me get ready. My mom and I both wore the same size shoes so I had my pick of high heels to wear with my dress. It was a red straight line dress with spaghetti straps. Mom had bought me a half bra to wear with it. The half bra was the same color as the dress and she had bought me a pair of panties that went with the bra. It was the nicest set of underwear I had ever owned.

"It's a shame no one but us will ever see it," Meg teased.

"Well, I'm sure not going to show it to your boyfriend." I said.

I was in a good mood, even though I was feeling twinges of guilt over going out tonight. Mom had not been looking good today. When I asked her how she was feeling she said. "I feel great! I made it to prom and tomorrow is graduation, so I made it to that too."

"Are you going to the ceremony tomorrow?" I asked. Lately she had been opting out of going anywhere much. She had been out maybe twice since my birthday.

"No, I don't think I'm strong enough, to sit in the wheelchair for all that time. It's going to take a few hours isn't it?"

"Yes," I said. "It's OK, maybe you shouldn't wear yourself out. I'll come right back afterward with Tony and Meg and we'll show you the video's we shoot."

"Do that tonight as well. Take lots of pictures. When I look at them it will feel like I was there."

"OK," I said.

Meg helped me with my hair and make-up. We found a good pair of shoes that I could actually dance in, not that I would have anyone to dance with. Then it was time for the photos. We went out in in the front yard in front of azalea bushes and took pictures of the two of us in our finery. Then we took pictures of each of us with our mother and our two mothers together. Mom did not get out of her wheel chair though.

Then a limo drove up.

Tony and Lance got out of the Limo. They had set me up with Lance Devers! We took more pictures and then we were off.

"How did they talk you into this?" I asked Lance.

"It didn't take much. I really wanted to ask you that day at the dog park. I just really got screwed up, especially after I called you that name. I'm sorry about that. I'm really sorry. I wasn't trying to mean."

"I know. It was just a mistake, right?"

"Yeah, and it almost ruined everything."

"But it didn't, here we are. On our way to . . . Where are we going? I didn't think the prom started until 8:00 P.M. It's only 6:00 P.M. now."

"We're going to take you out to dinner," Tony announced.

They took me to Hill's Fish Shack which was my favorite place to eat. My mom loved the stuffed mushrooms there.

"I love this place."

"I know, you're mom told us," Meg said.

"You just arranged everything didn't you?" I accused my best friend.

"Yeah," she said, turning it into a three syllable word.

I took pictures of the food, I took pictures of the four of us drinking 7-up out of Champaign glasses and making toasts to our future and our friendship. Then we left and went to the Hotel where the penthouse had been turned into a sparkling wonderland. We had our pictures taken as we entered and then we found the punch bowl. We circulated and chatted with people. Meg and Tony mostly did that. Some of the football players stopped Lance to chat with him, but he brushed them off quickly. He acted like he wanted to only spend time with me tonight. We found a table for the four us to sit, and that's when Tony sprang it on me.

"I have a room in this hotel tonight, after the prom we can go there and stay longer."

"You are a pig!" I exclaimed. I'm not going to any hotel room with you guys. You and Meg go, I have to go home and tell mom everything that happened."

"She's getting the memos," Meg said. "Besides, it's not what you think. Because of prom, the pool is going to be open all night. So I brought our swim suits, and we can go down and swim for a while, then we can get room service, since Tony's Dad is paying for the room, and then we can go back and sit in the hot tub. We can just pull an all-nighter."

"I can't." I said. "My mom."

"She said she wanted you to have fun, right? Well, who do you think gave me your swim suit?"

"She really does want you to have a good time," Lance said.

"OK," I told them just to keep the peace. But I still planned to ditch them eventually. I would stay until people started leaving for their after parties and then I would make an excuse and leave. I had some cash, I could call a cab.

We danced one really wild one to Baha Men, asking the age old question, "Who let the dogs out?" We were taking a lot of pictures of the four of us dancing. When the song was finished we sat down to rest and drank some more punch.

The crowd started to thin after that song. It had tired everyone out.

"Let's go downstairs to our room," Meg suggested.

"OK," Lance said. "Let's go."

We got in the elevator and Tony pressed the button for the 22nd floor.

The elevator started going down and that's when I felt it.

I can't describe it entirely, but it was kind of like a surge of fatigue washed over me. I instinctively knew that something had happened. I put my hands on the wall of the elevator, reaching for the rail. My knees buckled and I slid to the floor.

"What's wrong?" Lance asked.

"I have to go home."

"No," Meg said. "We agreed. You just got dizzy, it's a fast elevator."

"No, something has happened. I have to go."

"Well, OK, I'll take you home," Lance said. "We'll take the Limo."

"No, you guys stay. I'll get a cab."

"Don't be ridiculous," Tony said. "We got the Limo. We'll take you home in it."

"You shouldn't have to leave. You got the hotel room and everything."

"We got it for the whole night. We can come back once you go home and check on her. I'm sure she's fine," Tony said. "We'll be back in 20 minutes."

"No, you should stay. I'll get home, no worries, all right? I'll see you all tomorrow."

I pushed them out of the elevator when the doors opened at the 22nd floor and I went down to the ground floor. I had the door man call me a cab, and while I waited Lance came down in the elevator.

"I'll go with you," he said.

"No, I'll be fine. You stay and have fun."

"I really wanted this to be a real date," he said.

The doorman said my cab was waiting. I walked out the door and opened the back door to the cab.

"Wait," Lance said. He came and put his arms around me. He kissed me awkwardly on the side of the mouth. I pulled back from him and looked him in the eye.

"We can do that better," I said. So he tried again. That time it was perfect.

I smiled nearly the whole way home. Gave the cabby a huge tip and went inside.

I didn't get much sleep that night. I had too many phone calls to make. I did it all in a haze of active numbness. I called hospice and they sent me a counselor and a nurse. They cleaned up her body and helped me figure out what to do next. The counselor asked if I wanted a lock of her hair to keep. I said yes I did, so the nurse lifted my mother's head while the counselor cut off a lock of hair. She found a piece of ribbon in her bag to tie around it. I picked out a robe that Mom liked. And the nurse dressed her in it. Then I called the funeral home that was to do the cremation and they came and got her.

"Will there be a viewing?" the director asked.

"No, we've already said our good-byes," I told him. That was when the first tear dropped from my eye.

"You've been to prom, huh," the director asked me.

I looked down at my dress. "Yeah, I forgot I was wearing this."

"Do you want me to call someone to come here for you?" the counselor asked.

"No, I'm fine. I'll be fine."

"Are you sure?" she asked. But I knew I had things to do, so I didn't answer.

"Do I come and see you tomorrow?" I asked the funeral director.

"I remember your mom," he said to me. "She wanted everything taken care of so you wouldn't have to be too bothered about it. Why don't you come in on Monday? I'll have the cremation done by then and we can finalize things."

"OK, Monday. Good." I wrote a note. Go to funeral parlor Monday. "What time?"

"We open at 10." I wrote 10:00 A.M. on the paper.

My mother was rolled out of the house at 1:25 A.M. on my graduation day.

She made it!

Lance

I didn't feel like hanging around with Meg and Tony after Cathryn left. I was a little worried about her, but Tony kept saying she would be fine. I asked Meg if she would call her, and she did but didn't get an answer back.

"She must have gone to bed, turned off her phone." I left the pool about one in the morning and decided I'd had enough. "I'm going to go and let you guys enjoy the hotel room on your own," I announced. Tony acted like I was doing him a favor, but Meg thought I should stay and keep having fun.

"It's just no fun without her," I said.

"I know," Meg agreed. Meg was Cathryn's best friend. I knew she missed her too. I got a cab home as well and left the limo for the two of them to take home in the morning. Meg's parents had paid for the

Limo. Tony's parents had paid for the hotel room. But My Dad told me to treat everyone to dinner at Hill's Fish Shack. So it was a group effort.

I snuck into my house and my Dad was still up.

"You're home early," he said. "Heck, neither of your brothers showed up before dawn."

"Can I borrow the car?" I asked him. I wasn't going to stalk her. I just wanted to do a drive by to make sure nothing was going on at her house. I didn't know what I was expecting.

"Are you drunk?" he asked.

"No, we hadn't gotten around to raiding the honor bar yet."

"Not a drop?"

"Nope. I've been a good little boy," I said. He laughed, threw me the keys. I put my tie and coat on the back of the couch and unbuttoned a couple of the top buttons of the pleated shirt.

"I'll be back in about 20 minutes," I said. I drove over to Cathryn's house. There was no one there. And no lights were on in the house. I thought about going up to her door to see if she was all right. But I realized that that would cause too much commotion at 2:00 A.M. so I ended up just looking up at the house from the vantage point of my car. I thought I heard something, so I turned off the engine. I couldn't hear anything. It was dead silent. So I started the car and left.

The next day I slept until it was nearly time to go to Chrysler Arena. Graduation started at 1:00 P.M. and we were supposed to be dressed and lined up ready to make our entrance by no later than 12:30 P.M. But no one was taking attendance, not on this day. I found Tony and we were standing together when Meg came up to us.

"She was right," Meg said. "Cathryn was right. Her mom did die last night."

"What? That can't be," I said. "I went by her house last night after I left you. The house was dark, there wasn't any activity."

"She told my mom that the funeral director came and got the body last night about 1:00 A.M. and she turned off all the lights and cried until day break."

"Poor Cathryn," I said. I should have gone up and knocked on the door. Will I never do the right thing? Ever?

"She said she can't make it today, Mom called the principle and told him that she wouldn't be here. He asked if she wanted them to observe a moment of silence for Mrs. Kucher, but Mom said no. But I think we need to do something anyway. I think we better do a standing ovation or something. Mom told me that when she talked with Cathryn she said that she wouldn't have anyone to clap for her anyway so she wasn't going."

"That's bullshit," Tony said. "Come on, let's spread the word. We'll make them say her name and then give her a standing ovation. You shoot some video. Tell everyone to shoot video and send it to us. We'll hijack this celebration."

We spent the next half hour making preparations for the hijacking. Then it was all in place and the ceremony began.

One by one, our classmates went up to receive their diplomas. Meg and I got our diplomas and then we stopped in the isle so that we would be ready.

Before the ceremony we'd found the person who was supposed to be behind Cathryn, Kenny Kursch, and told him to stop at the bottom of the stairs to the stage. That would be our signal.

When the last person before Cathryn got her diploma, Meg and I made our move. I grabbed her hand and together we got up to the stage. I took the mike from the person making the announcements.

"Hello everyone, I said. I would like to first observe a moment of silence for the mother of one of our classmates, Mrs. Denise Kucher, mother of Cathryn Kucher, My girlfriend and Meg's best friend."

I waited for a count of ten and then said, "Cathryn's mother died last night while we were at prom. It was her wish that Cathryn be happy and enjoy herself. Cathryn is an A+ student who will be attending the University of Michigan next year. She has a successful dog walking business called Bow Wow Dog Walking and Training. She's the smartest and best person I know. Accepting the honor of receiving Cathryn's diploma is Meg Bennett on behalf of the Track team."

I began to applaud, everyone applauded as Meg walked up to get Cathryn's diploma. Tony was in the audience shooting video. Soon everyone was standing. I was the last one to stop clapping. Then I yielded the floor.

After the graduation we all went over to Cathryn's house to show her the videos. Mom and Dad, Tony and his parents, and Meg and her parents, were all there.

Dad ordered Pizza at mom's request. "Denise didn't have many friends so I don't know if there will be any food there."

I thought about when my grandfather had died. All the neighbors and family members brought food over to Grandma's house. Maybe Cathryn and her mom didn't have anyone to bring her a Tuna Casserole. But I was wrong. Some of the neighbors had stepped up and brought her over some store bought plates of cookies and cold cuts. I figured it was her clients.

Cathryn pulled out what she had and when the pizza arrived, we had a little sad feast.

Cathryn looked like she had been crying all night, and most of the day as well. She smiled at the standing ovation they gave her though. She looked at me sharply when I made my announcement that she was my girlfriend. She even commented, "Girlfriend huh?"

"Way to man up," my dad said and winked at me.

Meg looked sheepishly at Cathryn, "What about your Dad? Should someone call him?"

"I got a notice last week from the court saying that since I turned 18 he no longer had to send child support. So no, I don't think he cares anymore."

"He should know," Grace said.

"Yes," My mom agreed. "He should be called."

"I don't want to talk to him," Cathryn said. "I haven't seen him since I was in sixth grade. He doesn't call me on my birthday or on Christmas. He wants to forget I exist? OK, I want the same thing."

"But still, he should know that you're on your own," Jack said.

"I'm 18. My mom prepared me for this. She only had that last round of treatments so she would live long enough to make sure I was going to be OK, and I wouldn't have to go to Foster Care."

I looked over at my Dad and thought about his favorite way of shaming us boys into doing grown-up things. Man-up he always says to us. It was time for me to man-up. Stand up for my girlfriend, if I really wanted her to be my girlfriend.

"I'll call him. I know what to say," I said. She handed me her phone. I found the number for Don Kucher. I dialed it. A man answered the phone.

"Hello, Bow, what do you know?"

"It's not Cathryn. I'm her boyfriend, Lance. She wanted me to call you and let you know that her mother passed away last night."

"Is she there? Can I talk with her?"

"I don't think she wants to talk with you," I said carefully.

"Tell her I'm sorry. Tell her I'll come, I'll come help her."

"That's not a good idea," I said. "She's very strong, very self-sufficient. She'll be OK."

"I don't need him. I will not be the excuse he needs to leave his new wife and kids. Tell him to stay home with them, where he belongs."

"She said . . ."

"I heard her," he said. "Tell her that if she needs me to, I'll continue the child support payments. They don't need to stop. Tell her I'll come out there and help her with the arrangements and find her a good place to live. Tell her . . ." I interrupted him.

"None of that is necessary. Cathryn is fine. She doesn't want your help."

"Tell him I don't need anything else from him. I just thought he should know. Hang up."

"She said . . ."

"Yeah, I heard her. Who are you again? Her boyfriend?"

"Yes," I said simply.

"Where she going to live?"

"Cathryn and Denise make a good plan. Everything is taken care of. You don't need to worry."

"So that's it? Stranger calls, tells me that my first wife dies and that my daughter is on her own but she'll be fine. What am I supposed to do with that knowledge?"

"Same thing you would have done if you didn't have that knowledge. Nothing."

I disconnected.

"Why did you even have his phone number?" Meg asked.

"Because of this. Because of this thing right here. If he sent me a gift I wrote him a thank you note. So I never talk with him. Never have, not since he left. He sends me a card on my birthday and he sends me a $25 gift card to Meijer's on Christmas. He probably would have stopped sending me child support years ago except that his wages were garnished by the court and sent to me automatically every month. It never amounted to much. Mom paid our health insurance and her life insurance premium with that money and what was left we blew on clothes for me and shoes for both of us, since we wear the same size shoes."

"So what did you buy from Meijer's," Meg asked.

"Dog food."

I couldn't help it, I laughed. It was so like her.

Friskey, the little dog, had been going back and forth between Cathryn and all the other people in the room, picking up little tidbits of leftovers that people gave him. He had climbed up onto the couch next to my mom.

"What about this guy? Are you going to keep him?"

"He was my Mom's dog. I don't know why she kept him. I think maybe she wanted me to have a companion when she died. But now that I'm legally an adult I think I'll keep doing dog rescues. I have room for them." The house she and her mom shared was on a large lot with a field behind it. There was plenty of room to raise dogs in this neighborhood.

"So you're really going to stay here?" My Dad asked.

"Yeah, my mom figured it all out. The house is paid for, I'm going to have an income from both her pension, and her life insurance policy, and for a little while, while I'm in school I'll get Social Security Death benefits as well. That should cover everything, and if it doesn't I'll find a roommate."

"Oh, I'll be your roommate!" Meg said at once. "I'm going to Community College in the fall. I can be your roommate and that way my mom and dad will be able to help you out financially if you need more money."

"Wait a second," Jack said. "You don't even know how much we're talking here."

"I'm moving in tomorrow, and I'll have my money from the ice cream shop to live off of, and once Cathryn knows how much more she needs she'll tell us. Right?"

"You can live here rent free until I find out how much I'm getting from all the sources. Mom showed me how to do a budget, so I have enough money to pay the taxes and insurance when they all come due. It's pretty easy, I just have to save like $60 or $80 out of each pay check so I have enough to pay the big yearly things."

"Um, we know," my Mom said. "We all have to do that."

"See, I'm very prepared for this," Cathryn said. "The deed to the house is my name and the car is in my name. She wanted to make sure I wouldn't have to go through probate to get my inheritance. My name is on all her credit cards and bank accounts."

"She must have really trusted you," Tony said.

"What was I going to do? Run off and spend all her money on a trip to Europe? She raised me right."

"He just said that," I told her, "Because his parents wouldn't have trusted him with all that."

"She had to count on me. She had to make sure I was grown up enough because she knew this day would come."

As I looked around the room I saw all the parents looking at each other. All at once I knew they were comparing themselves as parents to Cathryn's mother.

"A parent's instinct is to protect their child from all of life's difficulties," My mom said. "That means something else entirely when you're a single mom and you know you're dying. I think your mom did a great job raising you."

"Thank you," Cathryn said and smiled.

No one seemed to want to leave that house. But eventually my parents decided there were other kids at home that needed their attention, and some dinner. So they made moves to say good bye and leave. I was determined to stay though until everyone else left. Pretty soon everyone else made an excuse to go as well.

Meg wanted to stay too.

"Are you really going to move in with me tomorrow?" Cathryn asked her.

"Yes, I definitely am!"

"Then don't you have some packing to do?"

Finally, we were alone.

"Cathryn," I said. "Will you be my girlfriend?"

"Oh, you mean I do have a choice?" she said. But she wasn't being mean. She was smiling. She walked up to me. "I would be proud to be your girlfriend."

Cathryn

Meg moved into my house the day after graduation.

She didn't want to sleep on the mattress that mother had died on, and frankly neither did I. It was just too weird. I couldn't do it. So for the first week we slept together in my double bed. I had some money that was in mom's account but I didn't want to spend it because I didn't know how long it would take for me to start getting the rest of the money from the other sources. Her pension check was due in about another week. Mom had worked it out so that I would get that source of income until I was 25.

As soon as I got the pension check in my bank account, Meg and I went out and bought a new mattress for mom's bed. They hauled away the old one when they delivered the new one. So I moved into my mom's room and Meg stayed in mine. We took all her clothes to St. Vincent de Paul, at least all those that we didn't want. She had some really cool t-shirts and sweatshirts. I wore her diamond engagement ring around my neck on a chain. And of course, I kept all of OUR shoes.

Tony was at our house daily but he didn't sleep over. Meg wouldn't let him.

I continued walking dogs and training them. Over the summer I made enough money so I could afford the tuition for the first semester at Michigan. I got a huge check in the mail made out to me from mom's life insurance and I called the banker at once, so he could put it in the trust fund. It was so simple, and I now had a reliable income every month. Tony thought we should blow some of it on a new boat, or a party or something. But I just shook my head. Kids!

It wasn't until I started school that I got my first check from Social Security. After that I made out my budget and found that Meg and I could live very well. We went grocery shopping together and split on the final bill, that way we wouldn't argue over whose yogurt we were eating.

We each paid for our own phones and personal shopping items like toothbrushes and make-up. But if we both used something, like our monthly pads or toilet paper, then we just bought that stuff with the grocery money.

It took us a few weeks to figure out this system, but we got it ironed out eventually.

And then of course once in a while we got a little help. Our boyfriends took us out to eat or we would come home and there would be a bag or two of groceries on the back porch that Grace had come over to give us.

Lance came over every day. He helped with the dog walking. He figured he had to walk Clyde anyway, so he became my first employee. I paid him under the table. I loved Clyde and I didn't want him to leave when Lance said he had to go home. Lance was working at Best Buy over the summer on the Geek squad, which, it turned out, was a great job for him.

Lance was reinventing himself and really came out of his shell. He had told his father that he wanted to be an astrophysicist, which made Lance into his father's favorite son. And I was his mother's favorite child as well because I came over every day on my dog walks and got Clyde. But that was for purely selfish reasons. Clyde was an eye catcher. People who needed my services saw how well Clyde behaved with me and hired me on the spot.

Lance and I went to Orientation together at Michigan and learned what we needed to know about the campus. Growing up in Ann Arbor didn't clue us in to half of what we needed to know about maneuvering in a big university. We sat down Friday night after the five day orientation and talked about it.

"I should have gotten into the dorm," Lance said. "I didn't realize what a stigma it would be to live with my parents."

"Just rise above it, Lance. It's not that big a deal. You're saving your parents and yourself thousands of dollars each semester."

"I know, but it comes with a meal plan and man, all you can eat! I can eat a lot."

The dogs all came around our feet at the mention of eating. "Go away," I told them. Some of them did as told.

I went down to the Shelter to sign up for dog rescues again once I started school. Rodney met me in his office to take my application.

"You'll be great at this," he said. "You still have that big sheltered kennel in the back of your house?"

"Yes, I do. And the backyard is totally fenced in so they can run loose when I'm home. There is a double gate as well so that even if we get an escapee from one gate, they won't get past the second one."

"Smart!" he told me. "I knew you'd be good at this back when we rescued those little Golden pups two years ago."

"Oh yes, I so wanted to adopt one of those. They were so cute. I just wanted to love them up and down."

"You know, I won the lottery for one of those pups. She's my bright girl, Becky. She had pups of her own earlier this year. I still have two of them. Do you want one?"

"How much?" I asked. I had Friskey but he liked staying indoors when there were bigger dogs in the kennel. He was Mom's dog, and he had never gotten over her death. Plus he was getting on in age. He was already greying around the muzzle when we got him. He had been left out in 20 degree snowy weather with no water or food for more than three days before he was rescued. He never quite managed to recover entirely. He would stand at the door and check the weather in the winter and only reluctantly leave the house.

"All the help you and your mom have given me, I'd be totally ungrateful if I charged you for her."

"Her?" I asked.

"Yes, her," he smiled. "You know, pure bred Goldens sell for sometimes as much as $1000 per pup. You could breed her and make enough to keep your student loans down."

I sighed. "I would love to have her, but I have to give you something."

"OK, here's what I'll take. You be my trainer, a job for which I will pay you a decent wage for the hours that you spend here. And give my little girl pup a good home. That's my final offer."

"No no no no no," I said. "I'm supposed to be giving YOU something. So instead you tell me two more things you're going to give me, not fair!"

He chuckled. "I've never met anyone like you, Cathryn. I need you to be part of this operation. You have skills that are too valuable."

I couldn't believe he was saying all of this to me. "But . . ."

"Furthermore, your Mom always told me that you have almost a sixth sense about placing dogs with people. I trust you to make those kinds of decisions. I don't want you to worry about telling someone they can't have a particular dog. I trust you to know if it's a good fit. And if there are any disputes, I'll be on your side."

"Wow, thanks!"

I went over to his house later that week to look at the five month old pup. She wasn't fully grown yet but she was already as big as Friskey. I took her home the next day after going out to buy her a pink leash and collar, and her own dog bed and bowl.

Friskey, Clyde and the new Golden, who I named Maxine, were the three main dogs in my pack. Of course I was the alpha dog always. Whenever I got a client with a dog problem, or should I say whenever I got a dog with a people problem, I would bring him home for the day, or for a few days to see if we could work out his problem here. Then I could observe his home environment and reintroduce him into his home hopefully having taught the humans something as well.

At the time of this conversation, I had two dogs that were boarding with me, and so there were five of them of varying sizes vying for our attention. It was here, while surrounded with dogs and with Lance by my side that I felt the most lonely. I sniffed.

"What's the matter," Lance asked.

"Nothing," I said.

"Come on," he said. "I'm here."

"I miss my mom."

"She would be so proud of you. Look at you, you've get a successful business, you are taking care of the bills, you are doing everything she knew you could."

"I know, but there is so much I want to say to her, to ask her, and to talk over with her. I just miss her so much." I began to cry in earnest then. Lance held my head against his chest and the dogs all came and climbed in around me, cuddling into me and Lance. When I looked up I saw that he was crying too. I cried for a good long time that night. But afterward, things looked a lot brighter.

Lance

I shed high school and my false persona of a jock like Clyde shed's his fur. I had spent a lot of time at Cathryn's house getting to know her. I wanted to know everything about her. She had a vague notion as to what she wanted to do with her life and it involved dogs and using them in the medical field to detect disease and to treat it as well.

Her thinking bordered on cutting edge philosophy and I wasn't sure if there was any validity to it but she and her mom had always had dogs, and so, I thought, maybe she knew something that the rest of us didn't. At any rate she had vague theories that needed to be explored.

Dad paved the way for me to go into the science department at Michigan and talk with the top Physicist there. I was put on the path that I wanted to be on. During the course of the discussion this scientist said that he would become my student adviser if I wished. I told him I would be thrilled and honored, two words that NASA taught us kids to say! So in an effort for him to get to know me, he asked me if I had a girlfriend. I told him happily about Cathryn. How she was going to Nursing school this year, but in the future how she hoped to be able to get into medical research and maybe do some experimentation on training dogs to detect certain diseases. He said he would like to meet her as well. Maybe he could get her involved in the research project of one of his colleagues. It sounded very similar.

"She has to get her nursing degree first," I told him.

"Why?" he asked.

"Because she doesn't have any parents. She's on her own. She wants her nursing degree so she can get a good paying job to support her future schooling."

"Smart girl. What if I can arrange for a scholarship?"

"That easy?" I asked doubtfully.

"Of course it isn't that easy, but if she has the interest in this topic there might be a way. Holistic Medicine of that sort is coming into vogue. We should make an appointment to talk with her and my colleague."

I did just that. It didn't take much talking at all to get Cathryn to take a meeting with the man. He showed her around their facility and she was impressed by the fact that there were no inhumane experiments being performed on dogs.

"This is a totally humane research," he assured her. "We want dogs to be our partners, not our test subjects."

"I have that same philosophy. My mom and I did dog rescues before she died."

"Oh, and what does your Dad do?" he asked her.

"I don't have a Dad, there was a sperm donor, but he's not in my life."

"I see, so how old are you?" he asked.

"I'm 18, I own my house and car and I run my own dog walking and training service."

"Really? You are just the kind of person I need. And you plan on getting your R.N. as well?"

"Yes. I was doing that mostly as a safety net though. I can always make money as an R.N."

"No, no, I understand," he said. "I think you should get your R.N. I could make a case of hiring you as an R.N. and make it a work study kind of thing. You could work with the dogs and then be the liaison to work with patients in a hospital as well and train the dogs in the hospital. Yes, this could work. Yes yes yes! Please let me be your student adviser."

"Of course, I'd love that."

Meanwhile, my student adviser and I walked along behind them as we toured the facility. I looked at him and he nodded. "I thought they might be a good match," he said.

"She was a 4.0 student in high school. I bet she could handle a double major, Research Science and Registered Nursing," I said.

Cathryn turned to look at me. "Wow, really? Do you think I can handle that?"

"Bow Wow," I said. "I think you can handle anything."

She lifted an eyebrow and smiled at the use of my new pet name for her.

I thought my life sucked. Then I met Cathryn and realized that as bad as I had it, her life was way worse and she did way more with it.

But now that Cathryn is part of my life, all of a sudden, everything is better!

About the Author

Cindy Koch-Krol was born in the Salvation Army Home for Unwed Mothers in Detroit Michigan. But her life went uphill from there! She is a writer, artist and crafter living in Traverse City, Michigan with her Husband, Jeff and Personal Chef, Jake.

Cindy enjoys the indoor sports of making quilts, knitting socks, and baking cookies. In the summertime she enjoys the outdoor sports of swimming, walking and basketry. She writes in front of her living room window looking out into her Fairy Garden and watching the wild life at her bird feeders.

This is her first Young Adult Novella.

Other Books By Cindy Koch-Krol

A Haunting at Mackinac—1920-Mackinac Island is the Vacation Mecca for affluent people from Detroit and Chicago. Alina, a young psychic in an age when spiritualism is in vogue, accompanies her guardian and his new wife on their trip to the Island. But on her first day she is bombarded with the voices of people and spirits all around her. She needs to learn how to control her gift to filter out the day to day inner voices of regular people, so she can better hear the ones who are calling out to her from the caves and crevasses of the ancient island itself. With the help of a gifted voodoo witch and her son, and an Ojibway Shaman, she stands a chance of gaining control of her own powers and using them to help the spirits trapped in the mystic vortex that surrounds Mackinac Island.

The Wolves That Watch—Nick's time in prison was both blessing and curse. He got his GED, he learned a trade and became a licensed auto mechanic, but prison was a harsh life lesson for him. Upon being released his mantra has become, "Never again!"

Sarah and her Mother both suffered trauma at the hands of a Narcisist boss after the death of Sarah's father. In order to escape their situation they are traveling to a tiny Northern Michigan town to stay with relatives and hopefully get a fresh start.

Nick and Sarah meet on the bus traveling between Jackson, Michigan and the small town of South Boardman. But Nick knows that he is not nearly good enough for Sarah. She's too young, too smart and too talented to waste her time on someone like him. But as he becomes more involved in his mother's Native-American culture, and continues to make better decisions, maybe he someday will be the kind of man who deserves a girl like Sarah in his life.

Northwoods—Tess is a travel writer and food critic fresh from journalism school in an era when newspapers are on a downward trend. She decides to take matters into her own hands and follows her heart and her intuition into the forests to find things to write about on her Blog and to sell to Freelance magazines. While traveling on foot through Northern Michigan, she befriends a dog who seems well trained and very smart. He likes her too. But later she finds out from a zoologist that he's not really a dog, he's a wolf. And still later, while traveling through Michigan's Upper Peninsula, she finds out from a tribe of Ojibwas that he may not be a wolf either, but something entirely different—something akin to the Dogman of Michigan.

Lost in the Woods—the second book of the Northwoods Saga, finds Tess and Kicky up against large primates in the northern forests of Minnesota.

While out walking through the forest Kicky is abducted by the strange creatures who seem to communicate through psychic means.

Trapped in his wolf form and cut off from his psychic connection to Tess, Kicky decides to stay with these creatures because of a small human girl who believes she is one of the troop. He wants to gain her trust so when he makes his escape, she will come with him.

But Tess is in a panic because when the psychic link between she and Kicky is severed, she fears he has been killed or incapacitated. She frantically searches for him. But is she searching for the a dead wolf, or a the living body of the shapeshifter she loves?

Border Babes—Patsy finishes the machine quilting on her latest project, turns it over to find she has sewn in a crease all across the back, so she goes into the bathroom and swallows every last sleeping pill she can find.

She wakes up in the hospital two days later surrounded by friends from her quilting club. One by one they tell Patsy their stories in an effort to distract her from her own traumatic childhood. But the memories she has to navigate are not entirely in the past. They are in the future, a future that will take all the courage Patsy can muster. Luckily her loving friends and family are there to help.

The Heart of Penfield Bay—Daniel grows up thinking that his destiny has been foretold to him in an amateur Tarot card reading when he was 14 years old. Ten years later he sees the woman who was foretold and falls in love with her at once. But is the rest of the reading true as well? Does she harbor dark secrets?

Clare's parents and Grandparents are killed in a car accident while traveling to see her graduate from Notre Dame. Riddled with guilt and unsure of the future, she packs up her disabled older brother and heads to the small town her grandparents called home, where she hopes to live a simple good life. But sparks fly when she meets Daniel. Then her Uncle calls to find out why she fled Chicago. She is needed to help run the family business, an endeavor that she had been groomed for by both her father and uncle.

Now she must choose between the simple life full of love and friendship, or the life she was meant to lead as the CEO in charge of a multi-billion dollar corporation which is innovating the field of clean energy. To complicate the issue, her Uncle wants to use the small town where she now lives as the prototype town for their products.

But Penfield Bay has a Heart—a secret that unites the entire town—and becoming a prototype town might destroy that beautiful place known as the Heart of Penfield Bay, unless Clare and Daniel can prevent it.

The Ghost of Dixboro—Based on a deposition dated December 8, 1845, by Isaac Van Woert, a carpenter, this is the story of his claims. It recounts ten times that he spoke with the spirit of a woman who claims to have been murdered. This book is a novelization of that story.

www.ingramcontent.com/pod-product-compliance
Lightning Source LLC
LaVergne TN
LVHW010107170826
845678LV00012B/2285